leaders,

fools,

and

impostors

Manfred F. R. Kets de Vries

leaders,

fools,

and

impostors

ESSAYS ON

THE PSYCHOLOGY

OF LEADERSHIP

JOSSEY-BASS PUBLISHERS
San Francisco, California

Substantial discounts on bulk quantities of Jossey-Bass books are available to corporations, professional associations, and other organizations. For details and discount information, contact the special sales department at Jossey-Bass Inc., Publishers. (415) 433-1740; Fax (415)433-0499.

For sales outside the United States, contact Maxwell Macmillan International Publishing Group, 866 Third Avenue, New York, New York 10022.

Manufactured in the United States of America

Library of Congress Cataloging-in-Publication Data

Kets de Vries, Manfred F. R.
    Leaders, fools, and impostors : essays on the psychology of leadership / Manfred F. R. Kets de Vries. — 1st ed.
        p.   cm. — (The Jossey-Bass management series)   (Jossey-Bass social and behavioral science series)
    Includes bibliographical references and index.
    ISBN 1-55542-562-3
    1. Leadership—Psychological aspects. 2. Executives—Psychology.
3. Interpersonal relations.   I. Title.   II. Series.   III. Series:
The Jossey-Bass social and behavioral science series.
HD57.7.K478   1993
658.4'092'019—dc20   93-17061
                                             CIP

Credits are on pages 225–226.

FIRST EDITION
HB Printing 10 9 8 7 6 5 4 3 2 1   *Code 9356*

A joint publication in

The Jossey-Bass Management Series

and

The Jossey-Bass Social and Behavioral Science

Series

Consulting Editors

ORGANIZATIONS AND MANAGEMENT

WARREN BENNIS

University of Southern California

RICHARD O. MASON

Southern Methodist University

IAN I. MITROFF

University of Southern California

to
Jack,
Larry,
Murray,
and Sudhir,
the friends with whom
I have shared my other lives

contents

preface

*Y*ears of experience have taught me that leaders and followers come in many shapes and sizes. The more leaders I encounter, the more difficult I find it to describe a typically effective leadership style. The same can be said about leader/follower relationships. The explosion of studies on leadership has made answering the question of which styles are preferable to others a remarkably difficult business. The most suitable response is probably that it all depends: obviously, different situations warrant different styles of leadership.

Not only is each specific situation in which leaders find themselves unique (here I am thinking about company and industry specifics as well as the expectations of followers), but the peculiarities of a specific national culture can also lead to great variations. To limit leadership characteristics to a list of a few common dimensions (as is done all too often in research on leadership) is an insult to the reader's intelligence. The lack of a definitive list does not imply, however, that there are no commonalities in leadership behavior. Leaders, after all, are part of the human race. Although some leaders may loom larger than life, certain general traits of human nature naturally also apply to them. The trick is to know how to make use of the universalities in order to increase our understanding of leaders.

Scope and Treatment

In deciphering broad patterns of human behavior, I have been greatly helped by the pioneering work of Sigmund Freud. Freud was the first to make us realize that we are subject to constraints in dealing with our environment. He pointed out that much of our perceived control over the world around us is only illusory. He highlighted some of the cognitive and emotional limits to rationality and demonstrated that we are never completely aware of what is going on in our surroundings—that certain things happen outside consciousness. One of Freud's more important contributions was his description of the role of unconscious motivation in daily life. His work helped us to understand the nature of causality in human functioning. It also demonstrated the existence of continuities between past and present behavior, between sleeping and waking life, and between health and pathology. Freud's insights have proved invaluable to our understanding of what makes people tick. In this book, I have tried to apply these insights to my personal research interest, the intrapsychic theater of leaders.

Background

Leaders, Fools, and Impostors is the product of many years of thought and reflection. The original inspiration for the collection of essays presented here came from some unusual encounters I had over the years with executives. Many of their stories originally seemed to me to be like the proverbial puzzle inside a riddle wrapped in an enigma. My confusion, however, was not without its benefits. In the first place, it made me curious; I wanted to delve deeper into the matter to make some kind of sense out of the material being presented to me. Second, it made me realize the extent of my ignorance and the difficulty of understanding certain situations.

I found myself having to learn to live with my ignorance, to tolerate ambiguity, and to prevent premature closure. Of course, keeping this feeling of openness is part and parcel of the clinical attitude, because there is always the hope that over time, as more data emerge, we will learn from experience. The expectation is that the patient, in various ways, will contribute the kind of material that will in turn provide insight into the various continuities that make for his or her specific behavior.

The encounters with leaders brought home to me the infinite ways in which human beings deal with stressful situations, the unique nature of our adaptive capacities, and the danger of getting stuck in vicious circles. In the final analysis, mental health comes down to the ability to choose, the ability to avoid being caught in a repetitive cycle.

Two different kinds of encounters made me aware of how Freud's continuities operate in leadership situations. First, there was my therapeutic experience. Learning from the patient is a continuing process that I find invaluable. It often makes me wonder who is teaching whom. For this experience, I am grateful to my patients. Second, the top management seminar (with its portentous title, "Leadership in Organizations: Exploring Your

Personal Style") that I have been teaching for some time at the European Institute of Business Administration (INSEAD) has provided penetrating insights into executive behavior. To spend three weeks (spread out over a period of six months) in this seminar with twenty senior executives is a powerful experience. It has made me understand the uniqueness of every leader's story—how each one has to carve out a personal path.

The purpose of *Leaders, Fools, and Impostors* is to present a view of the interactions of people in organizations that is more sophisticated and realistic than the one-dimensional and mechanical descriptions traditionally put forward by students of management. The book focuses on the psychodynamics of organizations and takes a clinical perspective, showing how unconscious as well as conscious internal processes can shape corporations, influencing many organizational decisions and corporate policies. It makes the point that rational approaches to management, which assume that human beings can be managed solely by logical, means-to-ends modes of organization, are mistaken. It demonstrates that corporate executives, like the rest of us, are not always rational beings; they may be driven by emotions, aspirations, or fantasies that influence the way they run their companies on a day-to-day basis. The book shows how irrational feelings of leaders and followers can infiltrate the entire corporate culture and management structure, why "normal" companies and their leaders can suddenly lose perspective—and money. This clinically oriented approach to management—recognizing the role of unconscious motivation, intrapsychic reality, and the limits of rationality—makes for a complex but at the same time authentic description of organizational life that will direct the executive to more effective problem solving and more creative leadership.

Leaders, Fools, and Impostors will appeal to five major audiences. First, the book will help business practitioners who want to deepen their understanding of what it means to run a business appreciate the extent to which their actions influence other people in the enterprise. Second, the book will help the student of management (whether business or public administration, political science, industrial and organizational psychology, organizational sociology, occupational psychiatry, or industrial social work) to acquire realistic knowledge of what organizational functioning is all about. Third, management consultants will profit from this book by going beyond symptom suppression in their consultation work to understanding the underlying causes, thereby increasing their effectiveness in organizational diagnosis, intervention, and change. Fourth, for the academic this book will provide an in-depth understanding of human motivation and action in organizations, making it possible to create more realistic models of organizational functioning. Finally, human resource professionals will benefit from this book in designing organizations that work, structures and systems that incorporate both rational and irrational elements that are more than figments of the imagination.

Overview of the Contents

The original stimulus for this collection of essays was a patient who brought me a number of mirror dreams. In interpretation I discovered that the mirror dreams signaled specific milestones in his development. They became a key to understanding the changes he was experiencing. Our mutual exploration whetted my curiosity; I wanted to learn more about the relationship between mirrors and people and the general role of mirroring in human development. So Chapter One was born.

Inevitably, my investigation of mirroring led to a need to know more about narcissism and the role of narcissistic behavior in leadership (Chapter Two). What are some of the developmental milestones in such behavior? What are the psychological pressures of leadership that encourage narcissism? What are the narcissistic traps leaders can fall into? On examining these questions, I discovered that one of the dangers of narcissism is the difficulty leaders have in letting go. It quickly became clear that power can be an addiction that is hard to give up. In Chapter Three I explore how leaders disengage or why they refuse to do so. I discuss the psychological issues that come to the fore when decisions about leaving a leadership position are made.

While the first three chapters of the book are concerned with general problems of leadership, the remaining chapters deal with problem individuals and the effect their behavior has on their followers. I became intrigued by the ways in which certain types of people occasionally encountered in organizations functioned. Chapter Four deals with the phenomenon of emotional illiteracy. Over the years I met a number of executives whose behavior struck me as rather mechanical. I became intrigued by the robotlike way they dealt with their environment and the inappropriateness of their reactions to stressful situations. When did this behavior begin? What led up to it? Do certain types of organizations contribute to it? My investigations were furthered by research into a clinical phenomenon sometimes called alexithymia—inability to deal with and recognize emotions.

In Chapter Five, I address another leadership issue that I became aware of in my work as a consultant to organizations. I often found myself placed in the role of the fool—not the fool as idiot, but rather the fool as truth sayer. On many occasions I have been asked to present certain painful issues, which have been dragging on for years, to the power holders in an organization. These issues have often been put on the back burner for far too long, where they are conveniently forgotten by executives afraid to bear unwelcome news.

Observing this sort of behavior made clear to me the need for countervailing forces to leadership, a sine qua non for the survival of organizations. Without such counterbalances there is a great danger that Louis XIV's statement *"Après moi le déluge"* will become a reality, and the organization will have a limited life span. The danger of pathology is always present. Many leaders, when they acquire a position of power and authority, lose a sense of boundaries, not realizing the impact they have on other people in the organization.

What inspired Chapter Six was a troubled encounter I once had in which I could make neither head nor tail of an individual's behavior and actions. I found I had to suspend my disbelief when dealing with him. Eventually, I realized that he had the personality make-up of an impostor. During the period I was in contact with him, I was almost seduced by the siren's call—I was aware of a strong wish to join his fantasies, to loosen my grip on reality, and to believe his stories, in spite of all the evidence that he was an impostor. This encounter led me to reflect on his manipulative behavior and in turn to investigate the more general questions of what makes impostors who they are and what makes people feel like impostors.

Stimulated by the news coverage of people with an abusive leadership style (specifically, Saddam Hussein and Robert Maxwell), I became curious about the factors that contribute to the abuse of power. How is it that some people can handle the power that comes with leadership, while others go off the deep end? This question became the starting point for Chapter Seven.

I conclude the book with some reflections on the requirements for effective leadership. What differentiates ineffective from effective leaders? What patterns can be identified? Inevitably, in dealing with these questions, I had to think about the elements of mental health. How does one differentiate on the continuum of health and pathology? What makes people feel good about themselves?

Acknowledgments

Although writing is a solitary process, books are not created in isolation. In certain ways books are the work of many people. As an old teacher of mine once said: "If you see a turtle sitting on a fence post, you know it didn't get there by itself." Many people have provided me with the impetus to write these essays, and as I mentioned earlier, the most important have been my patients and students.

Many of the chapters in this book were originally written as articles for such journals as *Human Relations, Journal of Management Studies, European Management Journal,* and *Organizational Dynamics.* The comments of the various editors and reviewers have been useful to me in elaborating certain parts of my analyses.

I would also like to acknowledge the support I have received from INSEAD's Department of Research under the direction of its associate dean, Yves Doz, assisted by Diana Mitchell. Their help in providing the resources for my research has been invaluable. Similarly, I would like to thank INSEAD's two deans, Claude Rameau and Ludo Van der Heyden, who have always been supportive of my work, which at times has seemed unusual for a business school to sponsor.

The retyping and correcting of the manuscript has always been done in good cheer by Elizabeth Florent-Tracy. No request for changes ever seems to faze her. For this I am grateful. The assistance of Ranu Capron (my secretary when I was writing the book) also proved invaluable. In her gentle way she played Cerberus to provide me with the time and space needed to do the writing. I do miss having her around.

Most of all, I want to thank my research associate, Sally Simmons. She has been more than helpful. Those of us who have written books know that at some point the excitement of writing something new is replaced by the tedium of rewriting the material one more time. She has been heroic in taking over where I left off modifying part of the manuscript. The process of rewriting and editing this book would have been difficult without her help.

Marcel Proust said in *Guermantes Way*: "All the greatest things we know have come to us from neurotics. It is they and they only who have founded religions and created great works of art. Never will the world be conscious of how much it owes to them, nor above all of what they have suffered in order to bestow their gifts on it." I do think that Proust had a point. There are often fine lines dividing health, pathology, and creativity. Many of the people in these essays, troubled as they may have been, were also great educators. By behaving and acting the way they did, they provided me with many insights. When I was in the process of becoming a psychoanalyst, one of my teachers told me that we really learn from only two kinds of people: children and those he termed romantically "crazies." Compared with the rest of us, these two groups tend to be much stronger in presenting their points of view, thereby furnishing us with a better under-standing of human nature. I hope that the reader of these essays about problems of leadership and problem leaders will take away some insights and put them to good use.

Paris, France   Manfred F. R. Kets de Vries
May 1993

the author

Manfred F. R. Kets de Vries holds the Raoul de Vitry d'Avaucourt Chair of Human Resource Management at the European Institute of Business Administration (INSEAD) in Fontainebleau, France. He did a doctoral examination in economics (1966) at the University of Amsterdam and holds an M.B.A. degree (1968) and a D.B.A. degree (1970) from the Harvard Business School. In 1977, he undertook psychoanalytic training at the Canadian Psychoanalytic Institute and was certified to practice psychoanalysis by the Canadian Psychoanalytic Society and the International Psychoanalytic Association. He is a practicing psychoanalyst. He is also a founding member of the International Society for the Psychoanalytic Study of Organizations and a member of its steering committee. He has held professorships at McGill University, the Ecole des Hautes Etudes Commerciales de Montréal, and the Harvard Business School.

Kets de Vries's main research interest is the interface between psychoanalysis, dynamic psychiatry, and international management. Other areas of interest to him are leadership, career dynamics, organizational stress, family business, organizational diagnosis, intervention, and change.

Kets de Vries is the author or coauthor of many books, including *Power and the Corporate Mind* (2nd ed., 1985, with A. Zaleznik), *Organizational Paradoxes: Clinical Approaches to Management* (1980), *The Neurotic Organization: Diagnosing and Changing Counterproductive Styles of Management* (2nd ed., 1990, with D. Miller), *Prisoners of Leadership* (1989), and *Organizations on the Couch: Clinical Perspectives on Organizational Behavior and Change* (1991). He is the editor of *The Irrational Executive: Psychoanalytic Studies in Management* (1984) and coeditor of the *Handbook of Character Studies* (1991, with S. Perzow). In addition, more than one hundred of his scientific papers have been published as chapters in books or as articles. He serves on several editorial boards. He is also a newspaper columnist. Kets de Vries's books and papers have been translated into ten languages. He has been a regular consultant on organizational design and strategic human resource management and has done executive development work with many U.S., Canadian, European, and Asian companies.

leaders,

fools,

and

impostors

OUR LEADERS, OURSELVES:

understanding
the leaders
we create

All the world's a stage,
And all the men and women merely players.
They have their exits and their entrances,
And one man in his time plays many parts.
—William Shakespeare,
As You Like It, act 2, scene 7

Those who go beneath the surface do so at their peril.
—Oscar Wilde,
The Picture of Dorian Gray

*a*ll community-dwelling crea-
tures need leaders; there is a leader in every pack, both of wolves
and of wolf cubs. In many countries where elections are regularly
held to select governments on local and national levels, we still
find titular, nonelected heads of state who inspire greater
affection and loyalty than the freely elected representatives.
When people are deprived of leaders, whether nominal or actual,
they will search for them, particularly in times of crisis and rapid
change. This fundamental need operates on a huge sliding scale,
from the wistful-cum-prurient interest shown in the royal

families of Europe by the media of countries that previously have deposed or eliminated their own monarchies to the spontaneous and fanatical support given to Adolf Hitler and the National Socialists in the Germany of the 1930s. The scale of consequences is correspondingly great, ranging from the harmless to the devastating.

An obvious implication of this need for leaders is a predisposition to follow; indeed, it might be said that human beings must do one or the other—lead or follow—in whatever social context we find ourselves. I am not referring only to the grander forms of leadership on the political scene or in big business; leaders and followers are basic archetypes of everyday life. At home, in the playground, at the office, in each situation we all have to deal with our position as either a leader or a follower.

We have always invested public leaders with heroic (or villainous) status. Traditionally, our heroes have been philosophers, writers, monarchs, generals, statesmen. Today's heroes, however, are often figures from the high-exposure world of corporate leadership, the men and women whose activities are beamed into everybody's living room by the television screen and whose successes and often spectacular failures are featured in every daily newspaper. We have only to think of the people from the world of business who have become household names in the recent past to realize how extraordinarily influential they can be outside their organizations. To give only two, widely differing, examples: the launch and subsequent collapse of John DeLorean's automobile business received a tremendous amount of media coverage, but that was nothing compared to the publicity DeLorean received when his ill-fated car was used as the time machine in Steven Spielberg's series of *Back to the Future* films.

Richard Branson, the entrepreneurial head of Virgin, is headline news whenever he undertakes one of his outrageous personal exploits, like crossing the Atlantic by hot-air balloon and speedboat. He and his company have also become irrevocably associated with some of the most consequential social and political issues—the AIDS-prevention campaign, environmental protection, and the rescue of hostages from Bahrain and Baghdad during the crisis in the Persian Gulf.

Our leaders, whether heroes or villains, are rewarded with reproductions of themselves in literature, newsprint, and analysis. The study of leadership itself, which is at least as ancient as Plato's *Republic,* continues almost to overburden the pages of historical, psychological, political, and business journals. Unfortunately, too many management theorists have reduced the study of leadership to a series of prescriptive rules, procedures, and models, and have failed to confront some of the most vital and interesting questions raised by the subject: what determines who will become a leader and who will not? What goes on in the inner worlds of our leaders? What is their intrapsychic theater like?

Leadership in action is characterized as much by its complications and subtleties as by its dramatic success-or-failure stories. These stories fill the bestseller shelves in bookshops and are much more attractive to those interested in leadership than dull, scholarly studies, notwithstanding the bestsellers' frequent superficiality and lack of conceptualization. Both sorts of publication—the theoretical study and the paperback potboiler—lack a pragmatic middle ground, where there is room to explore the psychological roots of leadership and the crucial dynamic of the relationship between leaders and their followers. This book attempts to provide that middle ground using the clinical paradigm to demonstrate that unconscious, out-of-awareness processes play an important role in organizational functioning. It draws extensively on my experience as an educator in a management school, a psychoanalyst in private practice, and a consultant to a number of corporations. Fundamental to the book as a whole is the consideration of the impact of leaders on their followers and what happens when this critical relationship malfunctions. For purposes of illustration, I give numerous examples from my clinical practice, from my teaching experience, and from historical documentation. I realize that engaging in psychohistorical exploration can be a risky endeavor; outside the consulting room, it is difficult, after the fact, to assess the validity of inferences made. The psychohistorical case vignette can never truly reflect the complexity of a person's life. However, I do believe that case studies can help clarify certain patterns of behavior. I hope the reader will bear with me and accept the historical examples as useful speculations.

chapter 1

THE LEADER AS MIRROR

Mirror, mirror on the wall,
Who is the fairest of them all?

I shall tell you the secret of secrets.
Mirrors are the doors by which death comes and goes.
Don't tell this to anyone.
Just watch yourself all your life in a mirror and
you will see death at work like bees in a glass hive.
—Jean Cocteau, *Orphée*

*I*n 1905, Freud published his famous case study of Dora, an eighteen-year-old girl referred to him as a hysteric. In it he describes a process in analysis where the patient acts out with the therapist patterns of relationships from the patient's past. Freud called this process *transference,* describing it as a "new edition" or "reprint" of the patient's emotional and psychological reactions to past experiences, revised and acted out in the present. In Freud's words, "a whole series of psychological experiences are revived, not as belonging to the past, but as applying to the physician at the present moment" ([1905] 1953b, p. 116).

Transference, while causing particular problems of detection in analysis, provides valuable insight into the situation being revived. In an everyday context, however, all of us act out transference reactions; indeed, most of our emotional responses are a combination of realistic reactions and "historic," or transferential, reactions to a given situation. These historic reactions originate in the earliest relationships we form—with our first caretakers, our parents—and the psychological imprints we receive then remain with us throughout our lives.

I have referred elsewhere (Kets de Vries, 1989, pp. 35ff.) to two modes of transference that are frequently seen at work in an organizational setting; they can be defined as *idealizing* and *mirror* transference. Both forms are complementary to each other and are essential to understanding the magic spell leaders cast on their followers. Followers have a tendency to idealize their leaders (an echo from early childhood, when the child wanted to be taken care of by an apparently omnipotent and perfect parent) in an attempt to endow the leader with quite unrealistic powers and attributes. It is a way of feeling protected and more powerful oneself. At the same time, the leader is mirrored in the eyes of his followers, and vice versa. Before analyzing how these forms of transference work in an organizational context, we need to look at their significance in general human behavior.

Personal Mirroring

The first mirror a baby looks into is the mother's face. As the pediatrician Winnicott (1971) says: "What the baby sees is himself or herself. In other words, the mother is looking at the baby *and what she looks like is related to what she sees there"* (pp. 111–112, emphasis added). According to Winnicott, the reflection that the child sees in the mother's face and the child's sensitivity to the changes seen there will very much determine the quality of the child's emotional development. This process, begun in babyhood, continues all our lives and explains why we continue to see our fears, desires, successes, and failures reflected in others. The quality of this interchange with the mother's face and the degree of emotional maturity in the developing child greatly affect a child's ability to test reality. At first, a mother's face reflects her idea of her child's perfection; as a child grows older, this mirror adjusts its reflection—the child no longer sees an uncritically adored image but a more reasoned perception of himself or herself as an individual. This adjustment is essential. Mirroring here is a two-way affair; it marks the creation of an initial sense of self and identity and is the foundation of the ability to form relationships with others.

The quality of the relationship between the mother and child, in which the roles of observer and observed alternate, is critical. The developmental psychologist Mahler (1967; Mahler, Pine, and Bergman, 1975) emphasizes the importance of phase-appropriate mirroring reactions in this relationship; the interplay of positive and negative, desirable and undesirable aspects of one's personality, helps define and validate the boundaries of one's sense of self—on the mother's part as well as the child's. There is, of course, enormous scope for distorted mirroring in this process: what the child sees and what the mother wants the child to see can be very different. This difference can take the form of an injunction not to recognize certain aspects of the parent ("Do as I say, not as I do"); such a distortion will be accompanied by a lingering desire on the part of the child to correct the image and may result in a sense of disorientation about one's self. In the words of one patient, "I really don't know who I am. I use other people, particularly my wife, to tell me. When I look in a mirror, I'm trying to see *who* I am. It's not a question of what I look like, but who is really me."

The degree of realism or distortion in these early emotional associations and formative experiences is not mere childhood trivia. The mirror does not slacken its hold on people in adulthood. As Shengold points out: "The mirror's magic, good and bad, stems from its linkage with the narcissistic period when identity and mind are formed through contact with the mother; the *power* of mirror magic is a continuation of parental and narcissistic omnipotence" (1974, p. 114, emphasis added). We all retain an indelible impression of our own perfection and the perfection of our parents. Kohut (1971) has termed these, respectively, "the grandiose self" and "the idealized parent image," and we all retain the desire to recapture that sense of wholeness and approval. We tend to seize any opportunities that promise gratification of that sensation.

The process of mirroring, and its link with the narcissism of the developing individual, is a fundamental human theme. It is enshrined in our popular mythology, in fairy tales (those deceptively naive stories that go to the heart of human psychology) and fiction, where the themes of reflection and distortion frequently appear. We think immediately of the magic mirror in the tale of Snow White, which dutifully assures the Wicked Queen that she is the "fairest of them all" and which is attacked by her in a rage one day when it unexpectedly tells her that her stepdaughter, Snow White, has surpassed her in beauty. In Oscar Wilde's novel

The Picture of Dorian Gray, the portrait of a beautiful young man gradually assumes all the outward signs of its subject's inner degeneration and becomes transformed into an image of monstrous evil and corruption. However, the most well-known story to incorporate the theme of mirroring is the myth of Narcissus, who preferred to take illusion for reality and killed himself for unrequited love of his own reflection in the surface of a pool. The soothsayer Tiresias had predicted that Narcissus would live to a ripe old age, provided he never knew himself. The appeal of this tale to our deepest instincts has made Narcissus one of the most potent symbols of our hopes and disappointments, embodying as it does the idea of a hopeless yearning for the unattainable—recapturing those oceanic feelings of complete fusion with the environment that originate in the earliest period of our lives. The longing of Narcissus encapsulates the process of mirroring.

The word *mirror* derives from the Latin *mirare,* meaning "to look at" and also "to wonder" or "to admire." *Mirare* is also the etymological root of the words *mirage* and *miracle.* The conjunction is appropriate because a mirror can be an instrument of both truth and distortion; indeed, it is difficult to think of a more effective device for our perception of fantasy and reality. Legend, folklore, myth, and superstition show that mirror magic can be both good and bad. Anthropologists (Roheim, 1919; Frazer, 1947) have described a huge number of mirror superstitions, emphasizing the frequent connection between mirroring and death.

Another regularly encountered belief is that a person's reflection is the image of his or her soul; thus, not surprisingly, in some cultures looking into a mirror is regarded as endangering the soul. As the psychoanalyst Elkisch writes: "Man's mirrored image first must have appeared to him as something graspable, real. But since actually it was unreal, namely, not made of stuff he could lay his hands on, he obviously felt that he was faced with his soul. And this soul being externalized might leave him and that would mean death" (1957, p. 240).

The metaphor of the mirror implies an awareness of multiple images of the self, the fateful division between private and public self-awareness. In this screen we look for what we want to see and try not to see what we fear to see: the meeting point between narcissistic omnipotence and reality. Frequently the sense of self—the moment when one begins to perceive oneself as a totality of physical fact and emotional awareness—has its origin in the powerful experience of perceiving and recognizing oneself in a mirror. Children will often play with their own image in a mirror, going through repetitive routines of disappearance and retrieval, which are magical ways of establishing the boundaries of the self. In the broadest terms, therefore, mirroring is an attempt to establish, maintain, and recover the boundaries of the self. Some support for this point of view can be found in therapeutic situations, where mirror dreams often seem to be triggered by the patient's desire for understanding and approval from the therapist, who in turn is trying to help the patient arrive at new understanding of the self (Eisnitz, 1961; Feigelson, 1975; Myers, 1976; Carlson, 1977). Carlson compares the mirror in these dreams to "the desperately sought 'gleam in the mother's eye,' . . . its reflective presence indicating an integrative capacity which is essential for the working through process and for the use of insight at especially stressful times" (p. 67).

An illustration may be taken from the case history of a middle-aged executive who turned to a therapist for help. This man had recently gone through a long-drawn-out separation from his wife, and he was seriously questioning the value and purpose of his personal life and his life at work. In addition, he was plagued with a recurring nightmare. In his nightmare he was walking along a dimly lit, ever-narrowing corridor. He felt a sense of panic as the walls closed in around him. Although he wanted to turn back, something compelled him to continue. Eventually, the only way he could move forward was by crawling; he ended up against an impassable wall that was covered by a mirror. When he looked into it, he saw his own face, horribly distorted. Then it began to disintegrate and ooze away. He would wake up screaming.

During the course of this man's therapy, he gained considerable insight into his problems and made a number of important decisions about his life. These coincided with the disappearance of his nightmare. A year later, he had another mirror dream, but this time entirely different. He dreamed he was sitting in the therapist's chair with the therapist behind him, and both were looking into a mirror. He smiled at the smiling face of the therapist and the image faded into a scene in which he and his mother were sitting beside a stream. He described vividly to the therapist the sense of tranquility that accompanied this dream. Here the image of the mirror accompanied this man's journey toward a more integrated sense of himself, symbolized graphically by the horrific sensations accompanying the earlier dream and the sense of peace and companionship that came with the second. We can infer that this difference points to a successful process of narcissistic-realistic adjustment in this particular individual's past, which left him with an active, enabling intrapsychic imagery.

Conversely, the recurring nightmare of another, very different person suggests an incidence where the primary process of mirroring had failed the developing child. The late Lyndon Johnson, former president of the United States, told his biographer Doris Kearns of a dream that plagued him during a period when he appears to have been in the throes of a severe identity crisis. Refusing to go to college, Johnson had run away to California, first working as a legal clerk for his mother's cousin—an alcoholic and highly unstable man—and then working for two years on a road gang. Kearns writes:

> *In this stormy period, [fifteen-year-old] Johnson suffered a recurrent dream that he was sitting alone in a small cage. The cage was completely bare...except for a stone bench and a pile of dark, heavy books. As he bent down to pick up the books, an old lady with a mirror in her hand walked in front of the cage. He caught a glimpse of himself in the mirror and to his horror found that the boy of fifteen had suddenly become a twisted old man with long, tangled hair and speckled, brown skin. He pleaded with the old woman to let him out, but she turned her head and walked away. At this point in the dream as he remembered it, he woke up, his hands and his forehead damp and dripping with sweat. He sat up in bed and then, not fully knowing what he meant by it but believing in it faithfully, he said half aloud: "I must get away. I must get away" [1976, p. 40].*

Given the nature of Johnson's dream, we can question his mother's capacity for reflective mirroring and her ability to provide a caring environment for her son. Her failure to do so might explain Johnson's later behavior, which appears to have been characterized by an insatiable demand for mirroring—that is, for a flattering reflection of himself—from all with whom he came into contact. He constantly had to be center-stage and attract attention from others, apparently lacking the inner resources to support himself and be alone. For him, in contrast to the troubled executive described earlier, the imagery of a soothing caretaker had never been properly internalized. Consequently, his sense of identity seems to have been fragile and in constant need of reaffirmation from others.

If, as I maintain, mirroring is a constant dynamic of our daily lives and relationships with others, the operation of that dynamic between leaders and followers in an organizational setting is critical. The various ingredients of the leader/follower situation—power, authority, hero worship, flattery, ambition, attention seeking—provide tremendous opportunities for distorted mirroring. Followers easily project their fantasies onto their leaders, interpret everything leaders do in the light of their self-created image of them, and fatally seduce leaders into believing that they are in fact the illusory creatures the followers have made them. Unfortunately, all too often some catastrophe occurs before both leaders and followers wake up from their make-believe world, leaving others to pick up the pieces. The financial policies of former U.S. president Ronald Reagan are a good case in point. Having inherited a budget deficit of $800 million when he took office, Reagan managed to increase it to $2.2 trillion by the end of his presidency. Many members of his constituency continued to negate the facts and persisted in believing in the possibility of a balanced budget. Reagan's success in facilitating a process—albeit with form rather than substance—whereby he mirrored the wishes of his constituency effectively cloaked his deficiencies as a manager of his country's resources.

To be a leader, of course, is to be more than a mirror or blank screen on which the desires and fantasies of others are projected. Scholars of leadership (Bass, 1981, 1985; Burns, 1978; Kotter, 1982; Bennis and Nanus, 1985; Leavitt, 1986; Tichy and Devanna, 1986; Kets de Vries, 1989; Zaleznik, 1989) have listed these attributes among those essential for leaders: the ability to articulate a vision of the future, to make choices (frequently painful), to use impression management to share one's vision with followers, to build networks, to empower followers, and to keep the perspectives of followers reality-based. These abilities must counterbalance the less tangible, attributional aspects of leadership: the extent to which followers wish to see certain qualities in their leaders and consequently ascribe meaning to their action or lack of action. Balancing these attributes is an applied version, if you like, of the reality-adjusted mirroring that the parent offers the developing child. The way leaders manage the mirroring process reflects their degree of maturity. The acid test is their ability to preserve their own hold on reality, to see things as they really are, in spite of the pressures from people around them to join their distorted mirroring game. In crises, however, given the human being's inherent potential for regressive behavior, even individuals with a great capacity for reality testing may engage in distortive mirroring.

These various observations about mirroring suggest that in the leader/follower relationship leaders seem to be defined partly by the desires of their followers. A great potential for distortion exists when leaders feel they need to act out the fantasies created by their followers. An organization in this situation is operating in a hall of mirrors, in which increasingly bizarre images are infinitely reflected. Wishes replace facts, and make-believe is substituted for reality. Most seriously, leaders can use their authority and power to set into motion entire operations founded on distorted perceptions, with serious consequences for the organization.

Mirroring in a Business Setting

Events in the Roltex Corporation (name disguised), an electrical appliances company, provide a good example of the mirroring process in action in an organizational setting. The Roltex Corporation, owned and operated by the Moore family, was founded by John Moore in the late 1940s. Eventually, two of Moore's three sons joined their father in the business. Peter, the eldest, looked after production and operations while the second son, Simon, became involved in marketing and sales. The third son, Bernard, worked in the company only a few summers while he was going to college. Independently wealthy, thanks to a trust fund set up by his father, Bernard eventually dropped out of college and spent most of his time traveling and playing music in a band.

Then, most unexpectedly, John Moore died of a heart attack. Like many other entrepreneurs, he had not created a clear line of succession. The consequences of his death were dramatic and reverberated throughout the company. After a period of considerable anxiety, much deliberation, and hesitation, it was decided at a family council—and later confirmed at a board meeting—that Bernard should become the new president. This extraordinary choice was made because both Peter and Simon felt that they were indispensable in their current positions and that any change in their departments would be unnecessarily disruptive while the company was in such a critical position. Because he had no expertise in any field, Bernard was paradoxically deemed to be best suited to look after general management. Initially wary because of Bernard's checkered background, most executives in the company believed they saw a remarkable transformation in him after he took over. They felt he grew into his new position quickly and were impressed by his accomplishments.

However, all was not well at Roltex, despite the general improvement in morale following Bernard's appointment. The firm began to lose market share rapidly, and profits began to slip. This deterioration was accompanied by a number of organizational problems and the loss of several key people. Simon was sufficiently worried to bring in a consulting firm to study the functioning of the company as a whole. Although he felt that his brother was extremely effective in his new role as president, Simon could not account for the drop in profitability and had his doubts about the appropriateness of company strategy.

The first thing that struck the consultants, who, as outsiders, did not share the anxiety prevalent in the company, was that Roltex was being run by a poorly trained individual who was astonishingly ignorant about even the most basic management practices. Unlike the company's own executives, they did not see the dramatic emergence of a gifted organizational genius. They saw an individual totally at a loss in his job. Where everyone else saw a pillar of strength, the consultants saw an anxious man who alternated between reluctant action and an acute sense of paralysis, engendered by his ignorance of his job. Furthermore, they noted that the few decisions Bernard did make were usually the ideas of some of his senior executives or, in a number of instances, were entirely imaginary because nothing was really done.

It also became clear that, on the rare occasions when Bernard took the initiative himself, he was guided by a few simplistic principles he had picked up over time. These principles seemed to be paranoiagenic (Kets de Vries and Miller, 1984), based on distrust and insecurity. For example, Bernard refused to share important financial information with his key executives on the grounds that he was afraid that employees would ask for salary raises if they knew how profitable the company was. This secrecy, however, hampered the making of informed marketing decisions. Bernard also embarked on misguided cost-cutting exercises to boost short-term savings, which proved costly in the long run. Nevertheless, many of his subordinates continued to attribute great wisdom to Bernard. The consultants were particularly struck by the fact that even his brothers joined in the reverential assessment.

The only reasons for Roltex's continued success were the company's existing portfolio of innovative products and the amount of energy put into the company by key personnel, including Peter and Simon. Undoubtedly, too, Bernard had had some positive effects on the company. His presence enabled the executive group to reaffirm a sense of control, if only illusory, over the company; they were very much using Bernard to reflect what they wanted to see. And he would usually, because of his ignorance of his environment, oblige by participating in the mirroring process. The consultants realized that allowing the present situation to continue would seriously endanger the company; however, given the attraction of this sort of distorted mirroring process, a considerable effort would be needed to break the spell.

Luckily, despite his insecurity and the misleading signals he was receiving from his executives, Bernard was still sufficiently in touch with the reality of his situation to realize its seriousness. He was aware that, in spite of his subordinates' fantasies, he might not be the right person for the job. Over time, he developed a relationship of trust with the consultants (a sine qua non for successful intervention) and admitted his sense of confusion, disclosing that he had never felt happy at having been made president. He was quite bewildered by events going on around him; he felt "completely out of it" and at times "unreal." He thought of himself as an actor in a play over which he had little control, and he was aware that he was stifling the company's progress. His real interest was still music.

It is difficult to define the nature of a regressive, distorted mirroring game for its participants. It is also difficult to stop it. In this instance, the consultants used a series of meetings with all three brothers to emphasize reality issues and demonstrate the destructiveness of inconsistent strategy-making alternated with a total lack of strategy. The consultants took great pains, while making these comments, to maintain a constructive, supportive atmosphere, as their efforts would have been completely undermined by the identification of a possible scapegoat. Change did not occur overnight. Gradually, however, the consultants' recommendations began to have an effect. The eventual solution to the company's problems was comparatively anticlimactic: Bernard decided to resign in favor of his brother Simon and left the business altogether, devoting himself once more to composing and playing music.

Coping with Mirroring

The history of the Roltex Corporation is a cautionary tale about the dangers of distorted mirroring. The constituencies of many companies fall into the trap of believing that their company is run by a gifted individual or, in the absence of real leadership, deny the reality of the situation and hope that, by magic, something good will happen. In the leader/follower relationship, we frequently see only what we want to see. The price of this process is faulty reality testing and dysfunctional decision making.

Leaders, as authority figures, easily reactivate historic responses from our childhood and turn into mirrors, helping us to integrate our perceptions of ourselves and helping us to consolidate a shaky sense of identity—particularly in periods of crisis. Many leaders do not object to this process. The admiring glances of their followers can be extremely satisfying. After all, we all have narcissistic needs. We should not ignore the fact that playing the mirroring game can have its positive side, as mirroring can, for a while, provide a much-needed adhesion, keeping a company together in times of upheaval and change. Its momentum can create a common vision and committed action, often with good results. Nevertheless, a healthy dose of insight and self-criticism, and of the ability to tolerate frank feedback from others, is needed to check the distortion in the mirroring process. Many leaders do not have that capacity, and the seductive pull from mirroring subordinates has led many of them astray.

Bernard was able to let go. He managed to break the mirror magic and free both himself and others from its fatal spell in time. All too often, however, catastrophe occurs before companies discover the destructiveness of their internal dynamics. Could other remedies or preventive measures be activated in a similar situation? Unfortunately, if the situation has degenerated to a critical level, all the usual safety measures a company may have built into its structure have long ago failed to operate. Perhaps the most effective treatment for an organization locked in a nonproductive, mirroring phase is the intervention of outside advisors—people who will hold up a different mirror, showing a different, truer image; their constructive interpretations can often help reorientate people who have lost their sense of direction.

chapter 2

THE INCOMPLETE SELF:

narcissism and the exercise of power

Worshipping a dictator is such a pain in the ass.
It wouldn't be so bad if it was merely a matter
of dancing upside down on your head.
With practice anyone could learn to do that.
The real problem is having no way of knowing
from one day to another, from one minute to the
next, just what is up and what is down.
—**Chinua Achebe,**
Ant Hills of the Savanna

Notwithstanding his occasional illusions of omnipotence,
the narcissist depends on others to validate his self-esteem.
He cannot live without an admiring audience.
His apparent freedom from family ties and
institutional constraints does not free him to
stand alone or to glory in his individuality.
On the contrary, it contributes to his insecurity,
which he can overcome only by seeing his
"grandiose self" reflected in the attentions of others,
or by attaching himself to those who radiate
celebrity, power, and charisma.
For the narcissist, the world is a mirror.
—**Christopher Lasch,**
The Culture of Narcissism

*O*ur reactions to the word *power* are the best indication of the ambivalent part power plays in human behavior. Few of us would deny its desirability, but we acknowledge contradictory feelings of unease and suspicion about the way power is directed toward us or, indeed, the way we handle it ourselves. The connotations of power touch on fundamental human preoccupations: strength and weakness, domination and subordination, control and submission—the exercise of one individual's will at the cost of another's. These connotations are disruptive and repellent and owe their particular force to the basic facts of being human—that we are born into dependency and that we must die. From the earliest moments of our life, our survival and growing sense of self are irrevocably linked to the use and abuse of power, both by influential individuals who have control over us and, as we develop, by ourselves.

Leadership is the exercise of power, and the quality of leadership—good, ineffective, or destructive—depends on an individual's ability to exercise power. To a large extent, the sources of a leader's power lie in the hierarchical authority given by the organization and the leader's professional competence, conceptual skills, vision and imagination, capacity for constructive interpersonal relations, and more personal characteristics such as charm, humor, and determination. But another attribute is required: a sense of individual potency. "Managing, directing, realizing one's visions, creating systems, and leading human beings in pursuit of a goal: all of these activities require that a leader have a certain feeling of potency" (Lapierre, 1989, p. 177). According to Lapierre, this feeling of potency is the result of the resolution within us of the archaic feelings of impotence and omnipotence that remain with us from the period of our earliest development.

The psychological health of developing children is linked to the appropriateness of their mothers' responses to their paradoxical state of helplessness and grandiose sense of self. The degree of encouragement and frustration children experience as they grow up and begin to measure the boundaries of their personalities has a lasting influence on their perception of themselves and others and the relationships they form throughout their lives. Any imbalance between their feelings of helplessness and the degree of protective nurturing they receive from their parents will be felt as a psychological injury. An inappropriate level of frustration, arising from their environment, handling, or ability to cope with discipline, will feed their natural sense of impotence, and they will commonly respond with feelings of rage, a desire for vengeance, a hunger for personal power, and compensatory fantasies of omnipotence. This dynamic continues throughout life, and if it is not adequately resolved within individuals as they grow up, it is likely to be reactivated with devastating effect when they reach leadership positions and learn to play the game of power.

Of course, power can be used for both good and bad, but the fact that it operates within these two extremes makes it an ambivalent factor in the field of human desires. Ambition, the need to make one's mark, the longing for conspicuousness, and the urge to take initiative and control are well within the bounds of the legitimate. However, it is the easy slide toward excess that is so worrying. History and literature have given us enough examples of the results of these excesses to justify our fear and suspicion of power vested in the individual. What happens when the game of power is played without first resolving this basic conflict between helplessness and grandiosity, impotence and omnipotence? What happens when power is abused? And does a sense of childhood injury inevitably produce a pathological attachment to power, or can it have a positive outcome in a constructive use of power?

Dealing with Childhood Injuries

Freud, writing in 1916 about some character types met in psychoanalytic work, called one group "the exceptions." Referring to Shakespeare's tragedy *Richard III*, Freud describes the sense of entitlement of Richard, Duke of York (later Richard III), his claim to special privileges and some form of compensation for the injustices he has experienced. Richard constantly invokes his physical deformity as justification for his "subtle, false, and treacherous" behavior (*Henry VI*, Part III, act 5, scene 6):

> *Then since the heavens have shaped my body so,*
> *Let hell make crook'd my mind to answer it.*
> *I have no brother, I am like no brother;*
> *And this word "love," which greybeards call divine,*
> *Be resident in men like one another*
> *And not in me: I am myself alone.*

Freud paraphrases the meaning of the famous opening soliloquy of Shakespeare's play *Richard III* ("Now is the winter of our discontent/Made glorious summer by this sun of York") as: "I have a right to be an exception, to disregard the scruples by which others let themselves be held back. I may do wrong myself, since wrong has been done to me" ([1916] 1953e, pp. 314–315). Whether their sufferings are real or imaginary, people with this sense of injury believe that the ordinary rules of conduct do not apply to them. They are permitted to trespass. They consider themselves chosen, entitled to special privileges. Destiny has given them a special mission. These convictions derive from the compensatory feelings of omnipotence they have fostered to shield their sense of helplessness. Their irresponsibility, recklessness, and license to overstep boundaries are justifiable because destiny, or fate, magically determines their choices: they never make a mistake themselves.

Erikson (1963) draws attention to the manner in which references to fate feature in the imagery Adolf Hitler uses in his autobiography, *Mein Kampf:*

> *His Reichs-German fairy tale does not simply say that Hitler was born in Braunau because his parents lived there; no, it was "Fate which designated my birthplace." This happened when it happened not because of the natural way of things; no, it was an "unmerited mean trick of Fate" that he was "born in a period between two wars, at a time of quiet and order." When he was poor, "Poverty clasped me in her arms"; when sad, "Dame Sorrow was my foster mother." But all this "cruelty of Fate" he later learned to praise as the "wisdom of Providence," for it hardened him for the service of Nature, "the cruel Queen of all wisdom."... "Fate graciously permitted" him to become a German foot-soldier.... When... he stood before a court defending his first revolutionary acts, he felt certain "that the Goddess of History's eternal judgement will smilingly tear up" the jury's verdict.*

> *Fate, now treacherously frustrating the hero, now graciously catering to his heroism and tearing up the judgement of the bad old men: this is the infantile imagery which pervades much of German idealism [pp. 305–306].*

Psychiatric literature has provided a wealth of clinical descriptions of Hitler's personality type or disorder. The particular problem with writing about Hitler's abuse of power is that the sheer scale of the horrors he inflicted on Germany and Europe makes any attempt to analyze his inner theater look at best feeble and at worst collusive. There is ample evidence from Hitler's own writings that he retained a sense of fundamental personal injury. He was raised by a hard, brutal man old enough to be his grandfather, who habitually battered his wife and children. Wanting only to become an artist, Hitler was prevented as much by his own lack of natural ability as by his father's opposition from doing so. During his lifetime, as well as after his death, many of those close to Hitler speculated on his sexual impotence, believed he was suffering from the effects of syphilis contracted as a young man, and described him as a "neuter": "The abounding nervous energy which found no normal release sought compensation first in the subjection of his entourage, then of his country, then of Europe. . . . In the sexual no man's land in which he lived, he only once nearly found the woman, and never even the man, who might have brought him relief" (Hanfstängl, 1957, pp. 22, 52). Probably Hitler's perception of adult authority as unfair and arbitrary, combined with his physical defects, contributed to a violent inner imagery of rage and hatred; unable to assimilate and resolve this imagery within himself, he projected it onto the external world. The results were the unparalleled horror of the Second World War, concentration camps, and sacrificial victims.

But will the consciousness of childhood injury necessarily result in such destructive projections of personality? Will it necessarily end in such aberrant ways of exercising power? The autobiography of the Swedish film director Ingmar Bergman suggests differently. Bergman reveals a childhood of inflicted terrors that he has nonetheless succeeded in reconciling through the creative and generative medium of the cinema.

> *Most of our upbringing was based on such concepts as sin, confession, punishment, forgiveness and grace, concrete factors in relationships between children and parents and God. There was an innate logic in all of this which we accepted and thought we understood. . . . We had never heard of freedom and knew even less what it tasted like. In a hierarchical system, all doors are closed.*
>
> *So punishments were something self-evident, never questioned. They could be swift and simple, a slap over the face or a smack on the bottom, but they could also be extremely sophisticated, refined through generations [1988, pp. 7–8].*

As Bergman recalls, the consequences of this upbringing were highly dramatic:

> *My brother tried to commit suicide, my sister was forced into an abortion out of consideration for the family. I ran away from home. My parents lived in an exhausting, permanent state of crisis with neither beginning nor end. They fulfilled their duties, they made huge efforts, appealed to God for mercy, their beliefs, values and tradi-*

tions of no use to them. Nothing helped. Our drama was acted out before everyone's eyes on the brightly lit stage of the parsonage. Fear created what was feared [pp. 139–140].

However, there was an interesting pattern in the punishment that Bergman was frequently forced to undergo:

There was . . . a spontaneous kind of punishment which could be very unpleasant for a child tormented by fear of the dark: being shut up inside a special cupboard. Alma in the kitchen had told us that in that particular cupboard lived a little creature which ate the toes of naughty children. . . .

This form of punishment lost its terror when I found a solution. I hid a torch with a red and green light in a corner of the cupboard. When I was shut in, I hunted out my torch, directed the beam of light at the wall and pretended I was at the cinema [p. 9].

If we take a rather reductionist view of career choice, we can see that much of the groundwork for Bergman's later film career was laid through his attempts to master these early experiences of terror. Bergman's use of the beam of light eventually turned into a fascination with the magic lantern. Through this constructive way of mastering his fears, he became one of the leading figures in film making, giving enormous pleasure to others. This is not to say that he has been able to overcome his inner demons completely. As he records in his autobiography, throughout his life Bergman has suffered from a host of psychosomatic disorders and other problems, including stomach ulcers, chronic insomnia, constant infidelity, and repeated nightmares about his ability to continue making films. Depressions descend on him like "flocks of blackbirds," and he has continued to use elaborate rituals to keep his various personal demons under control. However, at the same time, he possesses the ability to transform these rituals into creative endeavors, in much the same way that he used his colored torch to ward off the terrors of the punishment cupboard.

The Narcissist in an Organizational Setting

From these relatively dramatic examples, let's turn to an illustration of how an individual's unresolved sense of self, or unrealistic idea of potency, can affect the working of an organization. The situation and its consequences might well be recognizable to a number of readers who have seen similar influences operating to a greater or lesser extent within their own organizations.

Harry Langner (name disguised) came to me for therapy, suffering from severe depression and a number of stress symptoms following his forced resignation after only five years as president of the Telar Corporation (name disguised), an established company in the brand-name foods business. His appointment to the presidency in his early forties had been the climax of a dazzlingly high-flying career. His predecessor had personally picked and groomed him for the job, with the general approval of the board and company executives. What had gone wrong in the intervening period? Why had Langner fallen from grace so hard and so fast?

The qualities that the outgoing president and other company executives had particularly admired in Langner—his talents as a team player and his professed commitment to participatory management—had melted away the moment he became CEO. Many of those who had known him before his appointment said that he seemed to change into a different person overnight. He was universally criticized for increasingly following his own path and no longer listening to what others had to say.

As CEO, Langner immediately embarked on a number of expensive projects. His first scheme was to relocate the head office of the corporation from the north to the east of the country, ostensibly to be nearer the market. However, cynics within the company suggested that the real reason behind the move was Langner's desire to be nearer his country estate. A series of luxurious purchases followed, including two company jets to fly Langner and his top executives around the world, and a custom-designed yacht allegedly to be used to entertain business associates. In fact, the boat was used by Langner and his friends mainly to go deep-sea fishing.

Stating that the purpose was to streamline the company, change its rather traditional image, and make it more of a trendsetter, Langner undertook two major reorganizations within four years. The only visible results of the work of the armies of consultants hired during this time were a serious destabilization of the company, the loss of a number of valuable long-term employees, and significant problems with morale. A number of questionable, extravagant acquisitions followed without much thought to their fit with other parts of the company. Telar began to have losses for the first time in years, and its stock value declined rapidly.

In spite of the company's going into the red, Langner's

salary and considerable perks remained unaffected. He appeared to be unperturbed by the downward slide in profits, enthusiastically organizing a planning conference in a chateau near Paris when the company was in increasing financial difficulty. No expense was spared, including the chartering of helicopters to transport company employees and guests, excessive speaker fees for a number of politicians, and the hiring of a three-star French chef to supervise the catering. By this time, Langner's autocratic style and imperious way of acting had completely alienated the few of his original supporters who still remained with the company. Any illusions of frank interchange had disappeared; good ideas were ignored and withered away. Several high-level resignations were given, stock was selling at an all-time low, and a funereal atmosphere pervaded the organization. Langner was unapproachable, as impervious to the problems within his company as he was deaf to those executives who tried to reach him. The crisis came when Langner approved a low-interest loan to a company of which he was part owner. This conflict of interest gave the board the excuse it needed to ask for his resignation. Despite his protestations that he did not see any potential conflict because he did not occupy a management position in the second company, Langner was forced to resign.

Some weeks after, with his morale at an all-time low, Langner came to see me. It was his first experience of therapy, and he armed himself beforehand by reading fairly extensively on the subject. He made an immediate impression as he entered the room. Good-looking and meticulously dressed, wearing an Armani suit, Gucci shoes, and a Patek Philippe watch, he wasted no time in demonstrating his familiarity with clinical terminology. One of the first things he did was to pull out of his briefcase a number of newspaper clippings showing him photographed with well-known people from the worlds of politics and the arts. He had no reservations about talking about himself.

Langner recalled that he was always the center of attention while he was growing up. His parents showed off his looks, dressed him up, made him sing songs and recite when they had visitors. He retained vivid memories of people sitting around, watching and encouraging him to perform. He was always considered very talented, destined to have a great future. His mother persuaded his teachers to allow him to skip a year in high school. In retrospect, Langner sometimes wondered whether that had been a wise move because it put a lot of pressure on him and he lost friends as a result. He complained that his parents never seemed to care much about his own personal desires; they were more interested in outward symbols of success, like academic achievements and good looks.

Langner was a very good high school student and at graduation was listed in the yearbook as the person most likely to succeed. He went on to study at an Ivy League college, where he was shocked to discover that things no longer came so easily to him. To obtain good grades, he had to work hard for the first time in his life—a task made more difficult by the amount of time he spent with women. After receiving his M.B.A. degree, Langner's major problem was choosing one job from among the many he was offered. He was a most successful interviewee, finding it extremely easy to charm recruiters. His interest in the media and taste for glamor led him naturally toward advertising. He initially joined a subsidiary of Telar, where his contagious enthusiasm and self-assurance led to a series of rapid promotions.

After gentle prompting, Langner acknowledged some of the

darker aspects of his personality. He recognized that his relationships had probably always been somewhat lopsided. He took admiration for his work for granted, feeling he was entitled to it. However, he found it difficult to show real rather than pretended interest in the work of others. Lower-level executives who failed to show enthusiasm for his ideas quickly found themselves out of favor. Langner admitted that rousing his anger could be dangerous for someone's career. He mentioned two occasions when he had gone out of his way to put rivals in a bad light. Although he knew how to be subtle, he could also be vindictive. Langner elaborated at length on his talent for charming his superiors. He was good at displaying his best side, at playing political games. It had paid off. He had obtained the top job— for a while, at least. However, with the top job he lost his sense of boundaries. Somehow he had slid into believing that the normal rules of conduct no longer applied to him, that he would get away with any transgression. The game got out of hand. The havoc his attitude brought to the organization, where people felt damaged and diminished, resulted in its near bankruptcy.

The Narcissistic Style

Narcissistic personalities like Harry Langner's are frequently encountered in top management positions. Indeed, it is only to be expected that many narcissistic people, with their need for power, prestige, and glamour, eventually end up in leadership positions. Their sense of drama, their ability to manipulate others, their knack for establishing quick, superficial relationships serve them well in organizational life. They can be phenomenally successful in areas that allow them to fulfill their need for greatness, fame, and power. However, although a certain amount of narcissistic behavior may be necessary for organizational success, like everything else, it is a matter of degree. A moderate dose contributes to effective organizational functioning. A leader's theatrical quality, confidence, and purposefulness can be contagious. In a faltering organization, these characteristics may even create much-needed group cohesion, as well as alertness to internal and external danger signs. Furthermore, the manner in which many executives use their subordinates as an extension of themselves does not necessarily have to be viewed in a negative way. A positive side is that these executives let their followers share their vision and expertise, thus offering opportunities for learning and career advancement. Obviously, this kind of leadership behavior is particularly effective within organizations in crisis, where enthusiasm and purpose are needed to generate motivation and momentum.

Unfortunately, the sense of excitement such narcissistic individuals inspire is frequently only temporary; it easily wears off. Then the darker side of the excessively narcissistic personality can be seen. Although the narcissistic executive is usually heralded as a person with great potential, over time it becomes clear that something is lacking—the original promise is never quite fulfilled. For these leaders, power and prestige are more important than commitment to performance; their energy may be directed toward projects that are politically expedient rather than at long-term goals. Their main concern is the preservation of their own position and importance, and they are contemptuous of the needs of others and of the organization. Their uninhibited behavior, self-righteousness, arrogance, inattention to organizational structure and processes, and inability to accept a real interchange of ideas impair organizational functioning and prevent adaptation to internal and external changes. Their consequent exclusion of others from policy making, intolerance of criticism, and unwillingness to compromise inevitably have serious negative effects on the organization.

One of a leader's most important roles is to be aware of and to accommodate the emotional needs of subordinates. Leaders driven by excessive narcissism typically disregard their subordinates' legitimate needs and take advantage of their loyalty. This type of leader is exploitative, callous, and overcompetitive, and frequently resorts to excessive use of depreciation. This behavior fosters submissiveness and passive dependency, stifling the critical function of subordinates. Sadly, the executives themselves are rarely conscious of their reasons for behaving the way they do. Usually only the onset of serious personal difficulties—physical aging, career setbacks, marital problems, or an increasing feeling of emptiness in their work and their relationships—makes such people begin to wonder what is happening to them and why.

Langner displayed many of the characteristics of the narcissistic personality. The damage sustained to his developing sense of self during his childhood had resulted in an overcompensatory style of behavior. On a superficial level, his parents seemed to treat him well. He was the focus of their attention and enjoyed, thanks to them, a privileged life-style and prestigious education. However, he probably was never allowed the psychic space he needed to develop a cohesive sense of his own identity. His parents' disregard for his personal feelings and their concentration on his appearance and the outward signs of achievement and success reveal an indifference to the real nature of their child. They used him as a proxy in their own search for admiration and greatness. Their behavior created only the illusion of loving. As an adult, Langner lacked an integrated sense of self: only if children sense that they are valued by others for their own sake will they be comfortable in their own skin and acquire a sense of inner value and self-esteem. When this sense is lacking, an individual engages in compensatory struggles for self-assertion and self-expression. In Langner's case, reaching a leadership position had released and activated his unrealistic fantasies about his own importance and entitlement; he exercised the power he held in accord with these fantasies rather than in accord with the real situation within the corporation. The apparently disproportionate amount of damage his behavior caused indicates the danger that one individual's inappropriate exercise of power can pose for a large organization.

Controlling the Effects of Narcissism

As might be imagined, the narcissistic personality is particularly prone to the perils of the leader-as-mirror effect, in which followers believe they see in a leader the positive qualities they want to see in themselves. To be able to function as a leader, the individual needs a certain amount of narcissism. Unfortunately, the mere fact of being in a leadership position overstimulates narcissistic processes. Not everybody can handle that stimulation. Individuals and entire organizations can easily become locked into the regressive relationship patterns that accompany the leader-as-mirror effect. These patterns are inevitably exacerbated by a narcissistic individual's reduced capacity for self-criticism and ability to distance oneself from oneself.

Unfortunately, the conventional systems of safeguards,

checks, and balances that operate within a large organization often fail to pick up the danger signs of the narcissistic personality before damage has already been done. The overwhelming narcissism discussed here, and demonstrated in the case of Harry Langner, frequently emerges for the first time when an individual reaches a position of power or, often, only after that person has held power for some time.

Regrettably, there are no ready answers to the question of what can be done to limit the potential problem. Recognizing the phenomenon in good time is one solution, although, as I have indicated, such recognition is not always easy. In the end, the well-being of the organization will depend largely on the healthiness of the leader's outlook, self-awareness, and sense of personal equilibrium. Sir John Harvey-Jones, the ex-chairman of ICI, had a clear appreciation of the problem. He wrote in his autobiography:

> *There are . . . added hazards which go with any top job. I have referred many times to the dangers of sycophancy, and my fears of the effect of power. It is almost impossible to avoid contact with one, or more likely both, of these hazards to one's ability to see oneself and one's motives clearly. . . .*
>
> *Eventually you rely on your ideals, and the picture in your mind of the sort of person you would like to be, and would like to remain. I think it is necessary to have this idealistic portrait to which you aspire, tucked away where you can check up to see how far, like Dorian Gray, you are altering. It is possible, although very difficult indeed, to hang on to quite a lot of yourself, if you recognize what is happening in time [1988, p. 227].*

Sadly, not all leaders are this penetrating. Many are only too willing to tolerate sycophants. Some leaders may eventually begin to imagine that these reactions are their due and that they deserve this kind of attention. An antidote to such behavior is the kind of realistic pragmatism described so well by former U.S. president Harry Truman, who once said: "I sit here all day trying to persuade people to do things they ought to have sense enough to do without my persuading them. . . . That's all the powers of the president amount to" (quoted in Neustadt, 1960, pp. 9–10).

Truman might have been exaggerating about the limitations of his power, but at least he maintained perspective. His sense of self was strong enough to withstand the seductions that come with high office. As the politician Adlai Stevenson is reported to have said, "Flattery is alright as long as you don't inhale." The trouble is that people do inhale. Power is a powerful narcotic—animating, life-sustaining, addictive. The people who have it have generally worked hard to obtain it and are not overkeen to let it go. This addiction poses a completely different set of power-related problems for the individual and the organization.

LETTING GO OF POWER:

the emotional reckoning

The more you know the more you know how little you know.
Your frustration is finite and your ignorance is infinite.
The more you resolve your frustration at your ignorance,
and the more you repair the damage done in your life
that led to your disappointment in your ignorance,
the more you may be able to love your ignorance and woo it.
All new will come from what you are ignorant of now.
—Clifford Scott,
"Who Is Afraid of Wilfred Bion?"

*S*ooner or later, people in posi-
tions of power have to let go. The extent to which letting go is
a positive or negative experience depends very much on the
individual and individual circumstances. However, it can have
a devastating effect on people and can sometimes seem like a
violent act, whether it happens at a prearranged stage in life (at
retirement age), through voluntary or imposed redundancy,
through organizational or political coups d'état, or, at the
furthest extremes, through ill health or death. For leaders, the
relinquishing of power is especially difficult. The public recognition that accompanies their position is a major factor in their

lives. Retreat into the private sphere represents an enormous reversal. They have become accustomed to identification with an institution of great power, to the influence that they can assert over individuals, policies, finances, and the community. They are used to receiving constant reaffirmation of their importance as individuals and of their role as leader to others. They have reached the top and the question of What next? is a critical one.

The difficulty in letting go may explain why so many leaders insist on remaining in positions of power when they themselves feel they have accomplished all they can, are no longer happy with their own performance, feel isolated or empty or unfulfilled, and have exhausted the challenges and no longer have a clear sense of direction. I have named this phenomenon *the CEO blues,* the backlash that comes from having been in power too long. Those who become CEOs at a later stage in life have it somewhat easier, particularly when there is a mandatory retirement age. Working within a fixed timespan means they are less likely than those with an indefinite timespan to feel stale and unchallenged; the initial sense of excitement in the job may endure. But for CEOs who reach the top at a relatively early age, a long tenure can turn into a serious problem. Their own early success is a hard act to follow. They may find themselves, after a surprisingly short length of time, desperate to know what to do for an encore. At some point they need to be able to say enough is enough and decide that the time is right for someone else to take over the reins. According to Matt Goody, onetime CEO of Dekker Chemicals (names disguised):

> *I felt wiped out all the time and spent most of my energy sweating over whether other people would notice my*

exhaustion and lack of concentration—which made both problems worse. It wasn't a healthy sort of tiredness, the kind where a shot of adrenalin carries you through. I'd lost any sense of excitement. Everything became a chore. I sat through meetings but couldn't have told you the first thing about what we'd discussed if you'd asked me afterwards. I'd been so good, but I'd lost it. People did notice, of course. Gossip filtered up. I started to get paranoid about it, watching my back, avoiding certain people. I felt I was hanging on to the whole thing by my fingertips. I used to say to myself, "Hang in there, you've got years to go yet." I was terrified I'd used myself up so soon; there didn't seem to be anything of me left. Driving in in the morning, I'd have to fight the impulse to turn and head straight back home. When the company started to lose market share I knew my state of mind had to be responsible: at least, I couldn't see any way out, which amounted to the same thing. I realized I wanted to run away, but it was a while before I could see getting out in more positive terms, for me and the company. It was too much, too soon.

Getting out and heading in another direction are practical options for relatively young executives like Goody, who have peaked early in their career. However, older leaders, faced with the question of what to do next and knowing that the answer is retirement, have to confront a different set of problems. A retirement date brings them up hard against a number of difficult and painful realities. Sonnenfeld (1986) identifies these realities as the consciousness of loss: loss of optimism; possible loss of health, vitality, and work (a critical activity in life), which threatens one's belief in the future; loss of reputation; loss of public exposure and public contact; loss of attention from others, of influence, and of feedback. Awareness of these losses is frequently exacerbated by consciousness of what the individual has already lost, or sacrificed, on the way to the top—a fulfilling personal life; good relationships with spouse, children, and friends; and time to develop outside contacts and interests. Clinging to power is a way of avoiding the necessity of confronting these realities.

The existence of such personal conflicts is easily understood. However, there are other forces at work, more difficult to distinguish, buried deep in the human psyche. We construct many barriers to exit for ourselves. The most obvious and superficial—although by no means unimportant—are financial and social. Leaving before retirement age can have detrimental effects on pension entitlements, which compounds the loss of income. Additional pressure to remain may come from spouses and children, who are used to the perks and reflected glory that come with the job, or from the habit of socializing with those who have comparable disposable incomes. Yet these constraints, realistic though they may be, can often be less important than other, overlooked factors; the financial and social barriers to exit are only the tip of the iceberg. The crisis of letting go is founded on a hidden mass of psychological and emotional factors.

The Effects of Aging

The stage in life at which individuals usually attain a position of leadership and power coincides with the time when the effects of aging start to become noticeable. The mirror reflects the fact that time is finite. There are a number of obvious bodily changes—dental problems, wrinkles, graying hair, balding, the need for glasses or stronger glasses, weight gain, loss of physical fitness. Research has shown that facial appearance and the genitalia are of special importance to an individual's sense of self. Sexual problems, particularly the decline in sexual ability in men, can be especially devastating to self-esteem. As might be expected, these changes are accompanied by a welter of emotional reactions, such as fear, anxiety, grief, depression, and anger (Erikson, 1963; Atchley, 1972; Kimmel, 1974; Lowenthal, Thurnher, and Chiriboga, 1975; Vaillant, 1977; Levinson, 1978; Gould, 1978; Kets de Vries, 1980b; Butler, 1985). At this period also one starts to look at life as time left to live rather than as time since birth (Neugarten, 1964, 1968). Changes in one's relationship toward aging, increasingly dependent parents, the death of parents, and the strain and stress that accompany having children all take their emotional toll. The underlying issue is that one has to come to grips with one's own mortality (Jaques, 1965; Kets de Vries, 1980a). We have to face up to and dismiss the hidden but cherished illusion of immortality.

This assault—time's assault—on the self can reactivate the feelings of inferiority and the compensatory striving that are characteristics of childhood. In view of the heightened narcissism of many top executives (a combination of predisposition and position), the awareness of decline perhaps has a greater psychological impact on them than it has on other people. The realization of one's mortality through the aging of the body is the ultimate narcissistic injury. In the second volume of his memoirs, former French president Valéry Giscard d'Estaing describes with startling frankness the fear and unhappiness that the awareness of his aging brought him.

> *It was while I was President of the Republic that I started to lose my looks. This development had started earlier, but insidiously. I have never completely accepted the way I look: too tall a stature, preventing a natural bearing; the hips too wide just below the belt; and, during adolescence, as the photographs show, something sweetly soft about my face, weakening its structural lines.*
>
> *I started to lose my hair when I was very young. I first noticed it in the bathroom of a hotel in a little German Kurort, which was lit by a window in the middle of the ceiling. The light was falling vertically, and I saw in the mirror how the light went through the crown of hair (each strand of which I could see separately), and fell directly on to the scalp. It filled me with a kind of terror. . . .*
>
> *Like all of nature, like every animal, I am the object of a slow process of decay. . . . But even if I am its object, I refuse to be its witness and I try to avoid all its signs. I never look at myself in a mirror, except to shave, and even then I make sure that the light is as dim as possible. When I walk along the street, I take care never to look into shop windows which might reflect my image.*
>
> *During my seven years as president, whenever I was seated opposite a journalist or took a child in my arms in a crowd, I did not think for one second that they saw me as I had become. I was convinced that they saw me as I thought I had remained—a semiyoung man of thirty-five, with hair around my temples, firm and flexible muscles, barely hardened or matured by life, and only just rid of the*

physical softness of adolescence. I keep all my old suits. I go on wearing them indefinitely. As they hardly show the wear, they help keep me in the illusion in which I live—that of a body which the passage of time has not affected [1991, p. 110].

Self-consciousness about the deterioration of the body and a sense of defect can stimulate the search for substitute outlets. For some people—and CEOs are prime candidates, given the position they occupy—the wielding of power becomes an important substitute activity. Henry Kissinger, Nobel Prize winner and former U.S. Secretary of State, once hinted at power's compensatory relationship with sexuality when he said ambiguously, "Power is the greatest aphrodisiac." Kissinger was well aware of the sexual attractiveness of power to members of the opposite sex, but his comment also suggests the ability of power to turn on its holder, perhaps making up for a lack of direct sexual satisfaction.

A more explicit example of the perceived relationship between the genitalia or sexuality and power is illustrated by a tradition—a real anthropological curiosity—that existed in an Indian Hindu kingdom until the turn of the seventeenth century:

It had been the custom of the Maharaja of Patiala to appear once a year before his subjects naked except for his diamond breastplate (composed of 1,001 brilliantly matched blue-white diamonds), his organ in full and glorious erection. His performance was adjudged a kind of temporal manifestation of the shivaling, the phallic representation of Lord Shiva's organ. As the Maharaja walked about, his subjects gleefully applauded, their cheers acknowledging both the dimensions of the princely organ and the fact that it was supposed to be radiating magic powers from the land [Ross and others, 1982, p. 524].

The Experience of Nothingness

The sense of loss and personal vulnerability that accompanies aging can make the idea of letting go of power and responsibility particularly unattractive. Many leaders display great intentness, single-mindedness, and persistence in maintaining a power base because the isolation in which many of them operate can stimulate fear of the loneliness and depression that might follow the loss of power. The threat of becoming an overnight nonentity, the experience of nothingness, generates an enormous amount of anxiety. President Harry Truman confronted this threat candidly when he said, shortly after leaving office, "Two hours ago I could have said five words and been quoted in every capital of the world. Now, I could talk for two hours and nobody would give a damn" (quoted in Graff, 1988, p. 5). Estranged from others by both their position and their actions, perhaps lacking a strong marital relationship, largely friendless, leaders facing retirement may find few people to turn to for emotional support to counteract the fear of nothingness. The dread of this experience may prompt a leader to hang on to a position, even if doing so limits personal contact to people motivated by self-interest and sycophancy.

An illustration of the psychological stresses involved in the process of letting go is provided by President Lyndon Johnson.

Since early childhood, Johnson had suffered from nightmares about paralysis: "He would see himself sitting absolutely still, in a big, straight chair. . . . The chair stood in the middle of the great, open plains. A stampede of cattle was coming towards him. He tried to move, but he could not. He cried out again and again for his mother, but no one came" (Kearns, 1976, p. 32). Strokes were not uncommon in Johnson's family. His grandmother had been paralyzed from the neck down by a stroke and sat in a chair like the one in his dream. It is interesting to speculate how far Johnson's childhood terror of paralysis, demonstrated by this dream, influenced his later behavior and actions—to what extent his search for power was a compensatory reaction to his fear and dread of helplessness. The president of the United States is the most powerful person in the world. Two previous presidents, Franklin Roosevelt and Woodrow Wilson, had been paralyzed. Did the two images become mixed up? Later events suggest that they may have. In the late 1960s, Johnson realized that his time as president was running out. His health was suffering, he was embroiled in political crises, it was becoming clear that the Vietnam War was unwinnable with conventional weapons, and he could no longer depend on his usual congressional allies. The chances of his winning a second term were remote. As his presidency drew to a close, the old nightmares returned in different form:

> *This time he was lying in a bed in the Red Room of the White House, instead of sitting in a chair in the middle of the open plains. His head was still his, but from the neck down his body was the thin, paralyzed body that had been the affliction of both Woodrow Wilson and his own grandmother in their final years. All his presidential*

> *assistants were in the next room. He could hear them*
> *actively fighting with one another to divide up his*
> *power. . . . He could hear them, but he could not com-*
> *mand them, for he could neither talk nor walk. He was*
> *sick and stilled, but not a single aide tried to protect him*
> *[Kearns, 1976, p. 342].*

Johnson would wake so terrified from this dream that he was too afraid to fall asleep again and risk a repeat. He could soothe himself only by going through a specific ritual. He would get out of bed and walk through the White House until he reached the portrait of Woodrow Wilson. After touching the picture, he would be able to return to bed and sleep. It was almost as if Johnson needed to make this symbolic gesture in order to reassure himself that he was still alive and not paralyzed, that it was Wilson who was dead. The symbolism of paralysis and his need to overcome it are significant indications of Johnson's mental state. Faced with the imminent loss of power, his delicate psychic equilibrium, which cost him so much to maintain, was wavering. Powerlessness meant paralysis, nothingness, and death.

The Talion Principle

One complicating factor for those faced with the prospect of relinquishing power is the fear, perhaps conscious, more likely subliminal, of reprisals. This *lex talionis,* or talion principle, derives from early Babylonian law and states that criminals should receive as punishment exactly the injuries they inflicted on their victims. This exacting retaliation, or rendering of an eye for an eye and a tooth for a tooth, has been the law of many societies throughout history. Although modern society has found other systems and forms of justice to compensate for injury, the ancient law of an eye for an eye and a tooth for a tooth still operates in the collective and individual unconscious (Fenichel, 1945; Racker, 1968). This subconscious belief is manifested in feelings of guilt and a general fear of retribution and by symptoms such as general anxiety, stress, depression, bad dreams, slips of the tongue, and the everyday language of revenge—"settling a score," "getting even," and so on.

However deeply buried this principle might be in a leader's subconscious, it can nevertheless form a substantial barrier to exit. Leadership involves the making of unpleasant decisions affecting the life and happiness of others; leaders cannot avoid intentionally or accidentally hurting some people some of the time. In view of the unconscious belief in lex talionis, it is unsurprising that leadership is frequently accompanied by paranoia. One example is the "management by guilt" syndrome (Levinson, 1964)—the tendency of executives to go to great lengths to sidestep or to smooth over conflict in order to avoid arousing anger in others. Leaders have to live with the expectation that someone will get even. Power is therefore a protective shield for them because the prospect of giving it up may be accompanied by the anxiety that retaliatory acts, perpetrated by those who have been hurt in the past, may be unleashed. More ominously, this anxiety can cause leaders to become caught up in an escalation of aggression. Their paranoid fear of retaliation makes them hang on to power and even resort to preemptive action, taking destructive initiatives to crush their opponents, or supposed opponents, even before there is any indication that they intend to retaliate.

The Edifice Complex

The fear of nothingness and the depression that accompanies it are accentuated by the need all of us have to leave behind a legacy. A common preoccupation of leaders is whether their successors can be relied on to respect the edifice they have built. It can be said that many leaders suffer from an "edifice complex." The fear that their legacy will be destroyed can motivate them to hold on to power for as long as possible. On a more fundamental level, leaving behind a reminder of one's accomplishment can be equated symbolically with defeating death. A continuing personal presence, whether actual or influential, can be an expression of a leader's personal difficulty in facing mortality, the inescapable necessity of letting go in the final sense.

The retiring leader, already buffeted by taxing emotions, facing an uncertain future for the first time in perhaps many years, has also to resign the vision or dream that has not only a personal motivation but also the driving force behind an entire organization. Furthermore, the leader may have to witness the systematic rejection of this vision by emerging leaders and be considered part of an inferior past, with no place in an alien future. Sonnenfeld (1986) identifies this as a crisis point: "When a new leader and a new dream are selected, the departing leader is left with a deflated sense of purpose since his purpose was fulfilled through the mission of the group. . . . Chief executives lose personal ownership over their own dream. As community property, it becomes critiqued, modified, adopted and ultimately discarded by the organization" (pp. 326–327). The challenge for the departing CEO, writes Sonnenfeld, is "to provide future opportunities for others who are blocked by the leader's mere existence" (p. 324). This positive challenge will be met if leaders can look back positively over their own career: "The more central work is to one's life goals, the more painful retirement is to someone who feels unfulfilled by [his or her] late career. Retirement can come to symbolize the forcible loss of a dream. At the same time, the review of one's record of achievement may provide one with a sense of contentment and satisfaction. The key is whether reachable goals have been met" (pp. 313–314).

If this reconciliation and acceptance are absent, it is all too easy for envy and anger to be generated. The retiring leader "may become angry at the 'selfish' younger generation, the ungrateful society, and the aging process itself, which threatens to erode a lifetime of building" (Sonnenfeld, 1986, p. 328). Generational envy—envy of the next generation—is common in organizational settings, with senior managers acting vindictively toward younger executives. The bitterness they feel at not having succeeded where the younger manager might succeed may induce them to set up traps and impediments to block the younger person's career. Their strategy can frequently be subtle: under the guise of giving the newcomer ample opportunities to prove himself or herself, they create parallel excuses for handicapping that person's progress. The drama that often accompanies management succession is a clear example of the working of these processes, particularly in those instances where potential "crown princes," ostensibly groomed specifically for the leading role, come to a bad end, having aroused the envy of their bosses. The succession dramas around people like Armand Hammer of Occidental Petroleum, Peter Grace of W. R. Grace, and William Paley of CBS may contain elements of generational envy.

The Process of Retirement

Loss of status, loss of recognition, loss of income, physical aging, and emotional stress: the connotations of letting go can seem overwhelmingly negative. Organizational culture and societal pressure frequently reinforce this negativity. It is clear that the problems of letting go have to be addressed on both an individual and an organizational level. Organizations are notoriously negligent in this regard. The individual on the verge of retirement is all too often abandoned to sink or swim, with no help or preparation from the organization. And too often people sink into bitterness, resentment, and depression through their own inability, or unwillingness, to face up to reality and prepare for letting go.

Howard Morton (a pseudonym) was a leading executive with a group of companies trading under a number of household names. His experience of letting go reflects many of the negative and damaging effects lack of personal preparation can have.

> *Well, of course I didn't want to go. Nobody ever does. They might talk a lot of rubbish about looking forward to retirement, but they're only trying to make the best of it.*
>
> *They had the cheek to offer me early retirement when I was fifty-seven. I thought it was a joke at first and couldn't believe it when I realized they were serious. They didn't push it once I made it clear how I felt. Then when my sixtieth birthday was coming up, they suggested I might like to reconsider. The human resources people had spent God knows how long preparing an in-house brochure on retirement strategy, and I remember them handing it to me as if it was some kind of prize. I made up my mind right*

then that I was going to stay on as long as I could. Nobody else knew as much about the business as I did. I thought they were ignoring everything I'd done over the years. I mean, I hadn't put all that into my work just to turn it over to some business-school graduate with a silly haircut because the human resources people thought I should.

I didn't think about retirement at all. Towards the end, I cut down the amount of traveling I did, but that was because the company decentralized a lot of operations and much of what we handled went directly to the regional offices. I didn't feel any more tired at sixty-five than I had done during the previous fifteen years. At times I felt a bit out on a limb. Nearly all my colleagues had gone and my division—like the rest of the company—was full of much younger men. They seemed very cliquey and I didn't have much to do with them.

I was very friendly with the outgoing CEO. We'd joined the company at the same time back in the 1960s. Our wives were friends and we all met socially. He stayed until his sixty-eighth birthday, then came in twice a week in a consultancy capacity for a further fifteen months. I assumed I'd do much the same thing; at least, I certainly didn't think that at sixty-five that would be it, finish, the end. When nobody said anything about consultancy, I mentioned it myself, and that's when they dropped the bombshell about dismantling the division. They tried to do it nicely. The VP Human Resources said it wouldn't be "viable" anyhow once I left, the company was getting behind the regionalization policy and opening more offices overseas. But I got the impression they thought I was taking up space. I seemed to be the only person to whom it came as a surprise. I felt stabbed in the back.

I know I was bitter. I still am. It didn't help that I started to get ill for the first time in my life—just aches and pains, the doctor couldn't find anything seriously wrong, but I had to have a series of tests and got into a depression. I refused their offer of a leaving celebration; it seemed such a sham. Who was celebrating what? I regret that a bit now because I left under a cloud, after more than twenty-five years in the place.

That was three years ago. I feel better now. I'm off the anti-depressants and quite by accident last year I discovered a real passion for gardening. We've got a large garden but I'd never really done anything in it—just used to pay the gardener. Then last summer he was off with a bad back for several weeks and I took the place in hand. Now we're really making it into something special. It's practically a full-time job. Things are better with my wife as well. It was misery when I was first at home. She's an artist, very wrapped up in what she does, and of course there's no retirement ceiling in her kind of work. I don't think she understood what I went through when I retired. It was ironic that the same week I left the company she had her first major solo exhibition. We're the same age and there she was, getting all the accolades, still pushing ahead, when I felt pushed aside. We talked about it. It wasn't easy. Last month was my sixty-eighth birthday and she gave me an oil painting she'd done of my favorite part of the garden. I hadn't known she'd done it; it was a fantastic surprise. It seemed to round everything off, somehow.

Howard Morton has now come to terms with his position, but the cost was high. His personality contributed greatly to his problems, but they were exacerbated by the insensitivity with which his company dealt with him. Although their efforts to confront the issue of executive retirement had been well-meaning, they had not gone far enough to be effective. Contrast Morton's experience with that of another retiring executive, in much the same situation. Jerry Taylor (also a pseudonym) was managing director of a shipping subsidiary of a large multinational company:

> *When I was in my early sixties, the company was taken over and the parent company began intervening more in our operations. Shortly afterwards my old [managing director] left and the atmosphere changed overnight. I became increasingly unhappy with the changes and on my suggestion my early retirement (albeit only six months early) was accepted. My pension was unaffected, the company continued to pay me until my sixty-fifth birthday, and I received a small bonus.*
>
> *I'd begun thinking about how I'd manage my retirement at least three or four years earlier. I knew I'd have to try and structure life after retirement in the same way I'd structured it in business. I knew I'd need a certain amount of discipline (no lie-ins, for example!) and as far as possible I planned things in advance. I wanted to do some charity work and I had that lined up for the time when I left the company. I finalized all those details about six months before I finished work. I took a couple of courses on post-retirement. One was organized by the local authority, the other I paid for myself. The company didn't*

offer any counseling, but I always found the personnel director helpful on an individual basis.

As the time grew nearer, I had generally very positive feelings about retirement. I suppose I felt apprehensive about some aspects but basically I took it philosophically, if not 100 percent enthusiastically. The company's attitude helped; they were happy for me to work from home several days a week and didn't make me feel that I was in the way, or past it. I wasn't too bothered about the loss of responsibility and decision-making. I was most worried about having nothing to do, which is why I put so much preparatory effort into restructuring my life. I was prepared to manage on less income and in fact we moved to a smaller house about a year before I retired, as our old house was starting to need a lot of maintenance.

I knew the person who took over from me, not well, but enough to know he was a pleasant chap. We'd never worked together before, although I'd known he would be in the running for my job when I did leave. In the last few months, I took him around, introduced him to customers, did a certain amount of handover work with him. That didn't cause me any problem: it was the normal thing to do.

Initially, I did think about taking on another job, some sort of paid employment. I made some inquiries and talked to a few people. But with all our children and grandchildren living abroad, I knew we'd be doing a lot of traveling and that really ruled out that sort of commitment. We spend at least four months of the year out of the country. When we are in England, my voluntary work regularly takes up two mornings a week, with some occasional meetings on top of that. I work mainly with older people, arranging outings, driving them to hospital appointments, and so on, and do the accounting for a local hospice. Most of our friends are also retired, so we see more of them. I'm reading more, and enjoying it more, swim and walk a great deal, and go to the theater or to a concert at least once a week. We've also taken two major trips since I retired, one to India and, eighteen months later, a tour of the world, something my wife and I have always wanted to do. My wife and all my family were very helpful and positive about my retirement. In the end, we were all looking forward to it.

Now five years on, I can genuinely say that I feel contented, very much engaged with life. I've met many people who feel that they've lost a lot with retirement, but that's not the case with me. I did wonder before whether I'd feel resentful, whether I'd feel I was missing out, or left high and dry. I know plenty of people who do. Would I go back now? Well, a couple of years after I'd left, my old company approached me with the offer of some consultancy work. I was very flattered, very pleased; it did mean a lot to have been asked. But the office has relocated, and we travel so much. . . . It wasn't too difficult to decide that I'd have to turn it down.

In the end, the most important things for me were that I was both fortunate and determined: fortunate that I found it easy to adjust first of all to the idea of retirement, then to retirement itself, and determined that I was going to make it work. And of course I had my wife with me all

the way, encouraging me to see it as a new phase in life,
rather than as the end of something.

Not every company is going to be lucky enough to have people with Taylor's foresight and confrontational approach, and, of course, not everybody facing the necessity of letting go will have either the time or the inclination to prepare as he did. For Taylor, retirement was an event, and a positive one at that.

In most companies retirement planning is viewed as largely a personal decision, and management provides little or no feedback or guidance. In view of the effect leaders' and senior executives' departures can have on company morale, this policy is dangerously shortsighted. However, it may reflect a company philosophy that is equally blinkered. Organizations are tempted to ease out senior people at relatively early ages for several reasons. Early-retirement policies can be seen as a way to rejuvenate the organization, as an alternative to laying off people during downturns, as a way of saving money (after all, older people are generally more expensive to employ), as an alternative to firing because of poor performance, and as a way of unclogging employment channels in order to create promotion opportunities for younger people. However, early retirements can create critical shortages of experienced personnel, which in turn can have negative effects on morale and performance. Organizations have to face several major issues: how to recognize and maximize the value and quality of experienced personnel; how to anticipate and contain the emotional and psychological costs of retirement and redundancy; and how to balance the psychological needs of executives with good policy for the company. The development of strategies to meet these issues can greatly ease the stresses of letting go.

Retirement policy should be enabling, allowing executives to address the adjustments they need to make when counting down to retirement. One such policy is phased retirement, where individuals can control their own gradual reduction in working time. Phased retirement can have the additional benefit to the organization of encouraging experienced personnel to remain in an increasingly part-time capacity. The costs of retaining older executives are far less than recruiting, selecting, training, and motivating younger people with less work experience. By the same token, redesigning a job or retraining can motivate older employees and help exploit their continued value to the company. Cutting down hours, phasing in the company pension, job sharing, and working at home—the gradual process of letting go—can help to cushion the shock that might otherwise come with the abrupt leaving of work. The feeling of still being needed will only reinforce peoples' morale and promote a positive attitude toward the future. Companies that facilitate personal adjustment toward leaving give people the opportunity to look beyond work and enhance their quality of life after retirement.

If this plan seems too idealistic given today's economic and social reality, it might be useful to remember that sooner or later we are all going to have to confront our time to let go, with all the psychological weight that that moment of realization carries. Intelligent and sensitive organizational policy should recognize that necessity; room and time should be built into organizational culture to deal with it. And, just as important, we should beware on a personal level of the darker side of power holding—its ability to detach the individual from the realities of life outside, its diminution of a personal life, its tendency to warp the responses of both leader and follower, its propensity to enmesh a leader in isolation, its overreliance on external symbols of success rather than inner stability—and recognize the need, as Sir John Harvey-Jones put it, to "hang on to . . . yourself" (1988, p. 227).

chapter 4

DEAD SOULS:

understanding
emotional
illiteracy

*I can neither live according to models nor
shall I ever be a model for anyone at all; on the contrary—
what I shall certainly do is make my own life
according to myself, whatever may come of it.
In this I have no principle to represent
but something much more wonderful—
something that is inside oneself and is hot with sheer life,
and rejoices and wants to get out.*
—Lou Andreas-Salome, *Lebensrueckblick*

Kill me, I can't feel anything.
—Dennis Cooper, *Closer*

*i*n 1956, William Whyte pub-
lished *The Organization Man,* a now-classic work in which the
quintessential organization man is depicted as colorless, dull,
unimaginative, and afraid to make decisions—a creature far
removed from his direct opposites, the entrepreneurs and con-
quistadors of business. He is a character we meet in many other
places—in Sinclair Lewis's novel *Babbit,* for example, whose
eponymous hero sees his way of life as "incredibly mechanical":
"Mechanical business—a brisk selling of badly built houses.

Mechanical religion—a dry, hard church, shut off from the real life of the streets, inhumanly respectable as a top hat. Mechanical golf and dinner parties and bridge and conversation. . . . Mechanical friendships—back-slapping and jocular, never daring to essay the test of quietness" (1922, p. 323).

The inhabitants of other, similar wastelands have peopled numerous nonfictional studies, including Erich Fromm's speculations about the proliferation of the marketing orientation, a form of behavior that he maintains is typical of modern life. Fromm's market-oriented people have a shaky sense of identity and are exceptionally superficial and changeable. Their identity seems to be made up of the sum of the roles they are expected to play. "The premise of the marketing orientation is emptiness, the lack of any specific quality which would not be subject to change, since any persistent trait of character might conflict some day with the requirements of the market" (1947, p. 85).

This sense of depersonalization, automation, and emptiness comes across well in Alan Harrington's *Life in a Crystal Palace* (1958). In the "crystal palace" (Harrington's ironic metaphor for a large organization) everything is bland and mechanical. Life is deadening; conversation is merely a way of avoiding silence. Everyone automatically and completely accepts the organization's policies and procedures. According to Harrington, the crystal palace turns into a corporate theater where conformity rules, all the actors are interchangeable, and people do not dare to call attention to themselves.

In *The Gamesman*, Michael Maccoby presents a more subtle view of the "corporate man," whom he regards as one among many types. Maccoby sees such a person as essential to the functioning of the large corporation, adding to its strength because of a strong identification with the organization's goals and ideals. At the same time, however, Maccoby warns about the dangers of this person's excessive dependence on the organization: "Although the company man's work tends to reinforce a responsible attitude to the organization and the project, it may also strengthen a negative syndrome of dependency: submissive surrender to the organization and to authority, sentimental idealization of those in power, a tendency to betray the self in order to gain security, comfort, and luxury" (1976, p. 94). The cultural historian Christopher Lasch echoes this theme of conformity and dependence, which he believes is accentuated by the fact that "the corporation takes on the appearance of a total institution, in which every trace of individual identity disappears" (1978, p. 70).

All these descriptions beg the question of whether Whyte had identified a specific personality type in his organization man, or whether he had merely used the character as a device in order to satirize organizational life. The continuing appeal of Whyte's book and the popularity of its theme suggest that Whyte must have touched a sensitive chord among those familiar with organizational life. He may sometimes have resorted to stereotypes and oversimplification, but there is truth in his depiction, and his work has had enormous impact. Why do these patterns of conformity and dependence surface? Is there something within organizations themselves that generates this sort of behavior? What do organizations do to individuals? Are certain otherwise dormant personality characteristics likely to come out in the open in certain types of organization? Perhaps the issue should be addressed differently. Are people with specific personality characteristics attracted to certain types of organization?

Can organizations be viewed as protective shelters for people with particular personality traits?

Whyte left in-depth psychological speculation to others. But the time has come to take up where he left off. Given the importance of the behavior patterns he and others have described—insofar as they have a negative effect on organizational creativity and innovation—I want to look more closely at Whyte's organization man in the context of a recently recognized clinical condition called alexithymia, a word taken from the Greek and meaning "no words for emotions."

The Identification of Alexithymia

What sort of person could be described as an alexithymic? Have you ever met a person like the one described by this executive?

> *For years I worked with a robot. It would have driven me crazy to have him as a boss; he was bad enough as a colleague. Sometimes you didn't know whether to laugh or cry. I could give you so many examples. He had a son, a year or so older than mine. The kid got into a great school. I said, "You must be so proud of him." He said, "You gotta have qualifications." Another time, I knew he'd been to a function where a famous violinist—an idol of mine—was present. I asked him if he'd met him, and he had. I said, "What was he like?"—you know, real excited, and he said, "Small." Like I say, you didn't know whether to laugh or cry.*

The term *alexithymia* was first coined in the early 1970s by Peter Sifneos, a Boston psychiatrist working with psychosomatic patients. He used it to describe a condition in which individuals were unable to find words to describe emotions, habitually used actions to express emotion and avoid conflict, were preoccupied with external events rather than fantasies or feelings, and had a tendency to give tediously detailed descriptions of the circumstances surrounding events rather than attempt to describe their emotional reaction to the events themselves. Pursuing their research, he and a colleague viewed alexithymia as a kind of communication disorder (Nemiah and Sifneos, 1970; Nemiah, 1977, 1978).

Henry Krystal, another psychiatrist working independently with patients suffering from severe posttraumatic states, was coming to the same conclusion. He noticed that alexithymic individuals "are unable to distinguish between one emotion and another" (1979, p. 17), but "like the color-blind person, they have become aware of their deficiency and have learned to pick up clues by which they infer what they cannot discern" (1979, p. 18). Krystal observed that emotionally color-blind people are superadjusted to reality and can function successfully at work. However, he also noted that once one gets "past the superficial impression of superb functioning, one discovers a sterility and monotony of ideas and severe impoverishment of their imagination" (1979, p. 19). Krystal noted an impaired capacity for empathy among alexithymics, who characteristically treat others with cool detachment and indifference. There is an absence of the human quality in the relationships they form; love objects are frequently highly and rapidly interchangeable. Krystal's observations were supported by others, who reported being left with feelings of dullness, boredom, and frustration when dealing with alexithymic individuals (Taylor, 1977). Many other researchers and clinicians in the fields of psychiatry, medical psychology, and psychotherapy have recognized and confirmed similar behavior patterns (Brautigan and Von Rad, 1977).

One important clinician working with alexithymic people is Joyce McDougall, who identified the high degree of social conformity among alexithymics and applied descriptive terms like "pseudo-normality" (1974), "robot" (1980a), and "normopath" (1978, 1984) to their behavior. She argued:

> *Instead of some form of psychic management of disturbing affects or unwelcome knowledge or fantasies, the ego may achieve complete destruction of the representations or feelings concerned, so that these are not registered. The result then may be a super adaptation to external reality, a robot-like adjustment to inner and outer pressure which short-circuits the world of the imaginary. This "pseudo-normality" is a widespread character trait and may well be a danger sign pointing to the eventuality of psychosomatic symptoms (1974, p. 444, emphasis added).*

The origin of this behavior, McDougall speculates, is a particular style of parenting, whereby the mother tends to use the child as a "drug" (1974, 1980b, 1982a, 1982b) and is apparently out of touch with the child's emotional needs:

> *Infants constantly send out signals to their mothers regarding their wants and dislikes. Depending on her freedom from inner pressures, a mother will normally be in close communication with her infant over these signals. If internal distress and anxiety prevent her observing and interpreting her baby's cries, smiles, and gestures correctly, she may, on the contrary, do violence to the tiny commu-*

nicator by imposing her own needs and wishes, thus plunging the infant into a continuously frustrating and rage-provoking experience. Such an eventuality runs the risk of impelling the baby to construct, with the means at its disposal, radical ways of protecting itself against over-whelming affect storms and subsequent exhaustion [1989, p. 26].

Many other studies (for example, Krystal, 1979, 1982, 1986; Gardos and others, 1984) have supported McDougall's conjecture that the pathogenesis of alexithymia is created in the first and second years of life. A number of clinicians suggest that such mothers (and fathers) solve their own, often narcissistic, conflicts through the child, who becomes trapped in what may be described as an aborted symbiotic relationship whereby extreme dependence is artificially prolonged. The child is treated like an extension of the mother and is under her constant surveillance; the child's body is handled as if it were someone else's property. Furthermore, the father may even covertly encourage this type of situation in order to be spared a similar fate, fearful of what he perceives as his wife's engulfing qualities. This sort of mother is far from being what has been described as a *mère satisfaisante* (a satisfying mother) and instead becomes a *mère calmante* (a tranquilizing mother). Consequently, the child never learns how to feel at ease without being in constant contact with her. The child fails to internalize the *mère satisfaisante,* a necessary process if, as an adult, he or she is going to be able to manage without continuous external stimuli (Fain and Kreisher, 1970). Such overbearing treatment of a child can probably be explained as the mother's way of arriving at some form of restitution for assumed defects of her own.

Because separation is discouraged by the mother, any desire the child shows for exploration or any form of initiative is nipped in the bud. Predictably, this sort of treatment has grave consequences for later personality development. In alexithymic individuals, the ability to differentiate and verbalize emotions never develops properly; this inability to recognize emotions in turn impedes the construction of the highly complex matrix of emotional signals on which we all rely for daily functioning and without which emotions are experienced as dangerous, potentially uncontrollable forces. Alexithymics ignore the distress signals given by their mind and body. Their fantasy life may become stilted; they are out of touch with their psychic world. Moreover, given the state of dependence to which they have become accustomed, they may become addicted to external stimuli as ways of giving structure to their world, unable as they are themselves to resort to their own symbolic representations, fantasies, or dreams to work through mental conflict. They need others to tell them how they feel. In the case of these individuals, the general human tendency toward mirroring (seeing in others what we would like to see in ourselves) seems to have been carried ad absurdum. In McDougall's words, what they feel "will appear in the people [they are] involved with. They are [their] mirror" (1982a, p. 88). They attempt "to make substitute objects in the external world do duty for symbolic ones which are absent or damaged in the inner psychic world" (1974, p. 449). However, in McDougall's opinion such attempts are "doomed to failure" and will lead "to endless repetition and addictive attachment to the outer world and external objects" (p. 449).

In general, alexithymic people are preoccupied with the

concrete and objective; the use of metaphors, allusions, and hidden meanings is foreign to them, and they are slow to pick up on them. They tend to negate and deny the existence of emotions (Von Rad, 1983). Psychologically, they seem to be almost illiterate, lacking any capacity for empathy or self-awareness and resorting to action as a way of dealing with conflicts (Neill and Sandifer, 1982; Lesser and Lesser, 1983; Taylor, 1984). McDougall terms their behavior an "activity addiction": "a drug-like relationship to their daily work or to numerous other activities (which sometimes do not even interest them), with the unconscious aim of leaving no room for relaxation or daydreaming. These people are continually involved in "doing" rather than in "being" or "experiencing" (1989, p. 97). Given their capacity to negate and deny emotions, people with alexithymic tendencies do not experience, nor are they aware of, intrapsychic conflict. Their physical behavior can have a robotlike quality, accompanied by stiffness of posture and a lack of facial expressiveness. External details seem to be used as a way of filling their inner deadness. They have never been permitted to experiment with their own feelings. As a result of their upbringing, their "true self" (Winnicott, 1975) has never been allowed to emerge.

Some clinicians have differentiated between primary and secondary forms of alexithymia. Primary alexithymia is regarded as a specific character trait possibly caused by genetic neurophysiological defects (that is, a disconnection between the left and right hemispheres of the brain, caused by a commissurotomy—a deficiency in the transmission of messages from the visceral brain to the language centers of the cortex). In the development of secondary alexithymia, sociocultural factors may play an important role. Alexithymic reactions may develop after a particularly stressful event or series of events, or in extreme situations. Toward the end of his first year of imprisonment in Spandau, in 1946, Albert Speer described the growing degree of emotional numbing he was experiencing:

> *This afternoon I suddenly realized quite plainly that my capacity for feeling is atrophying as a result of the adjustment to prison life. Yet that alone makes it possible to endure the pressures of the situation. I might put it paradoxically: Loss of the capacity for feeling increases the capacity for suffering. . . . I must force myself to intellectual activity. . . . Only the narrowest and most banal area remains to me. I concentrate on the table in my cell, on the stool, on the markings in the oak of the door. I try to grasp these things as precisely as possible and describe them to myself. A first exercise in—Well, what? Certainly not in literary activity; but a test of my capacity for observation (1976, p. 6).*

Speer continued to apply this strategy of close detailed observation throughout his twenty-year sentence; twelve years later, he describes the hours he spent absorbing the precise appearance of some hawk feathers he had found in the prison garden (1976, p. 325). Similar kinds of emotional paralysis were experienced by concentration camp victims and veterans of the Vietnam War (Freiberger, 1977; Shipko, Alvarez, and Norrello, 1983; Krystal, Giller, and Cicchetti, 1986).

All the studies indicate that, as a communication disorder, alexithymia is relatively widespread. As with any clinical syndrome, however, estimates of its prevalence among the general population vary. For example, one study carried out among undergraduate students suggested that 8.2 percent of the men and 1.8 percent of the women could be defined as alexithymic (Blanchard, Arena, and Pallmeyer, 1981), although the validity and reliability of the instruments used in this particular study are questionable. But whatever the exact proportion of alexithymics in the general population, there is considerable confusion about the etiology of alexithymia. Is it a character trait or a situation-specific form of coping behavior? Is it the price that has to be paid for emotional labor and stress? Could it be both trait and state (Von Rad, 1984; Ahrens and Deffner, 1986)? No clear answer has been found.

Nevertheless, it is clear from the large body of clinical observations of the condition that an identifiable problem exists—whether individually or societally—in the management of feelings. The existence of a phenomenon like alexithymia underlines the importance of the capacity to feel emotion in the functioning of human beings and suggests that it is just as important as the capacity to see, hear, or smell.

Alexithymia is not an all-or-nothing phenomenon. On the contrary, apparently we are all potentially vulnerable to it to varying degrees. It seems to be a graded dimension with individuals occupying different positions on a scale of cognitive-affective experience and expression (Martin, Phil, and Dobkin, 1984). Our alexithymic inclinations may have an insidious influence on our perceptions and actions. To this extent, the resemblance of the alexithymic individual to Whyte's organization man is striking.

The Alexithymic Predisposition of the "Organization Man"

Consider the responses given in the following interview recorded between a psychologist (A) and a company executive (B).

A: What do you do?

B: I work in a data processing department.

A: Can you say something about your work?

B: I like the place. I like my office. It's rather big . . . in a corner. I get a lot of sun.

A: What can you say about the people you work with?

B: Not much. . . . I find it hard to describe what I feel about them.

A: What prospects do you have to get greater responsibility?

B: I don't know. A colleague of mine who used to work for me recently got promoted to a divisional job.

A: Did you get upset about that? After all, he used to work for you.

B: No, those are the breaks.

A: What is your relationship with your wife like?

B: Alright. We've been married for fifteen years.

A: Have there ever been any problems between the two of you?

B: She had an affair once with another man.

A: How did you deal with that? Did you feel hurt?

B: I didn't feel very much. When she told me about it, I said it was alright. . . . I think it's crazy, all this talk about feelings. What's important is to make a living.

A: How is your relationship with your wife now?

B: She sometimes screams at me for no reason.

A: Have you found out why she gets so upset?

B: No.

A: Do you have children?

B: Yes.

A: Can you tell me something about them?

B: I have a boy and a girl. They're doing fine.

A: How do you feel?

B: I've had stomach pains for three years. It got worse, but I discovered that if I held myself in a certain position it hurt less. I managed until the ulcer perforated. Now I take pills and watch my diet.

A: What do you usually do when you're at home?

B: I watch television.

A: What was the last program you watched?

B: I don't remember. I usually forget the story line immediately.

A: Do you ever dream?

B: No.

A: Do you ever fantasize or daydream?

B: Not that I can remember.

A: Do you ever cry?

B: No.

A: Do you ever get excited about things?

B: No.

A: Do you feel anxious about being here?

B: My boss told me I might.

A: What thoughts do you have now?

B: I don't know. . . . None. What do you expect me to say? I find it hard to describe how I feel. . . . I'm not much of a talker.

Many years ago an astute observer of organizational life wrote of some of its characteristics: "The dominance of the spirit of formalistic impersonality, 'sine via et studio,' being without hatred or passion, and hence without affection or enthusiasm. The dominant norms are concepts of straightforward duty without regard to personal considerations. Everyone is subject to formal equality of treatment; that is, everyone in the same empirical situation. This is the spirit in which the ideal official conducts his office" (Weber, 1947, p. 340). Max Weber's description of the bureaucrat echoes the wooden, unemotional, and unimaginative responses and behavior of the alexithymic executive interviewed above. His answers show how little room he has for feelings and how, when asked how he feels, he tends to resort to descriptions of external events. As with many alexithymics, his behavior appears to be almost overadaptive. Behind the initial impression of excellent functioning, we discover the sterility of his imagination and the monotony of his ideas.

Large organizations can be extremely attractive to alexithymics because they provide an ideal opportunity for the individual to blend into the organizational culture. Many organizations offer environments that legitimize behavior that would be seen as strange in a different setting. In doing so, they give the alexithymic disposition relief, in that they provide some kind of structure. This structure helps disguise alexithymic behavior and provides a "containing" environment for the alexithymic character (Bion, 1961). Furthermore, if we accept the possibility of the existence of secondary alexithymia, as described above, we can see that certain types of organization possess the numbing quality that can activate dormant alexithymic tendencies in their employees.

Most of us have come across alexithymic individuals in management circles: polite people in suits, making all the right noises, whose company after a while creates a dreadful ennui; cold fish, whose interest in others is swiftly revealed as false; people who resolutely play safe and as a result function in an atmosphere of mediocrity—of ideas, performance, and results. Although many such individuals give the impression that they feel comfortable behaving as they do, the kind of stress symptoms they show (which often remain long hidden from themselves) suggest otherwise—as the alexithymic executive with the long-neglected perforated ulcer demonstrates. Alexithymic behavior is not only personally damaging; it can also have severe repercussions for the organization and the people who have to work alongside these individuals. Alexithymics are frequently extremely successful, particularly within large organizations where playing safe, making the right noises, predictability, and relative inconspicuousness are often rewarded. Many organizations favor predictability over maverick and innovative behavior because people who do not take risks do not make expensive mistakes. However, employing such people not only creates the possibility of providing entirely the wrong sort of role model for other executives but also contributes to a mediocrity, which drives out excellence.

Two types of organization seem to cultivate alexithymic behavior: the compulsive and the depressive. I have already described these archetypes (which are oversimplified here for the purposes of the present discussion) in earlier research (Kets de Vries and Miller, 1985, 1986, 1988). The compulsive organization is bureaucratic and tends to be inwardly focused. It usually has a rigid hierarchy, in which individual status is related to job title. The leadership dominates the organization from top to bottom, demanding strict conformity to rules and procedures. Slavish adherence to programmed, standardized, and routine practices is the norm. There is usually strategic reliance on a narrow, established leitmotif to the exclusion of other factors. Formal codes, ritualized evaluation procedures, and risk aversion combine to make any form of change an extremely difficult proposition. Companies with strong corporate cultures that are very rules-and-regulations oriented, like IBM, Philips, Fiat, and General Motors, display some of the characteristics of this organizational type. With these particular examples, however, the positive aspects of the organization appear still to outweigh the negative.

The depressive organization is in many ways similar, but it is in worse shape. It frequently drifts with no sense of direction and is often confined to antiquated, so-called mature markets. Its survival depends on protectionist practices, and it is characterized by extreme conservatism, a vague set of goals and strategies, and an absence of planning. Structurally, these organizations are bureaucratic, ritualistic, and inflexible. There is a leadership vacuum, a lack of motivation and initiative, and an attitude of passivity and negativity. Communications and market analysis are poor, so there is ignorance of market trends. The organizational climate is impersonal, with a prevalent fear of decision making and great resistance to change. After the death of its founder, the Disney Corporation went through a period when it was in a similar state. Many state-owned companies fall into this category, although they can often continue to operate in this way for considerable lengths of time because of government protection.

Both of these types of organization provide ideal camouflage for people with an alexithymic disposition because the expression of affect or emotion is not often readily permitted. Because of the engulfing nature of this sort of corporate culture, its effects on the individual should never be underestimated. Although other organizations may induce similar effects in their employees, none has that peculiarly numbing quality found in some compulsive and depressive organizations.

As a caveat, it should be mentioned that many organizations, particularly in the service sector, make a great effort to manage the emotions of their personnel. We have all grown accustomed to the meaningless utterances of flight attendants, bank tellers, and telephone operators—"Have a nice day," "Thank you for calling the Grand Hotel"—which are symptomatic of institutionalized behavior. The ability to manipulate the emotions and behavior of executives is frequently seen as a competitive advantage. Airlines like Delta and Cathay Pacific and entertainment companies like Disney World have gone a long way in this direction. At Disney World, for example, which prides itself on being customer-friendly, inspectors police customer relations and ensure that there is no breakdown in communications. Every employee has to undergo an indoctrination process, and elaborate manuals indicate what the company considers to be appropriate behavior in any given situation. These companies require employees to show the correct emotion at the right time, irrespective of their current mood. Some people resist this type of manipulation in order to retain a minimum level of authenticity and remain in touch with their own feelings; others are more suggestible and vulnerable to this type of emotional control. The tension that arises between authenticity and conformity can have considerable impact on people's emotional and psychological well-being.

How do people who do not have alexithymic characteristics function on a long-term basis in organizations where emotional manipulation is a central philosophy? The sociologist Arnie Russell Hochschild, in her book *The Managed Heart* (1983), worries that "the worker can become estranged or alienated from an aspect of self—either the body or the margins of the soul" (p. 7). She believes that those who identify with the job and do not recognize the contingent development of a false self (Winnicott, 1975) risk psychological burnout. Even non-alexithymics may suffer from emotional numbness if they are working in organizations that manage emotions in an intensive way. They may lose the ability to separate their own self from the role they are required to assume by the organization and become unable to distinguish their own feelings from the prescribed ones—in other words, they become pseudo-alexithymics themselves.

Individual Styles

Alexithymic behavior at the top can have serious organizational consequences. The detached CEO provides one example. However, we do not have to go all the way to the top to find this type of behavior. Certain kinds of jobs suit the alexithymic disposition very well. Two types of people, whom I have identified as the systems person and the social sensor, show a type of behavior that can also be observed in those with a schizoid condition (Kets de Vries, 1980b).

The Detached CEO

Occasionally top executives experience great difficulty in dealing with emotions. To protect themselves from emotional involvement, these people develop a detached style. Their emotional isolation, however, can have serious organizational repercussions. Quite apart from giving a sense of direction, a senior executive has to be a container of the emotions of subordinates. A good executive is something of a psychiatric social worker in this regard. Excellent executives will take the emotional pulse of the company on a daily basis because understanding the preoccupations of subordinates is a key element in motivating them. Inability or unwillingness to respond to the dependency needs of subordinates can create confusion, resentment, and aggressiveness (Kets de Vries and Miller, 1985, 1986, 1988). A highly politicized organizational culture may develop, where people turn from the business at hand to concentrate on protecting their own patch of turf, creating warring and uncooperative fiefdoms, and erecting barriers to the free flow of information. In such an organizational culture, it is unsurprising that the focus is internal, self-directed. A vascillating, muddling-through type of strategy can usually be observed, its orientation depending on whichever clique has managed to get the ear of the CEO.

In one organization, the CEO was described as "the Yeti, living at great heights and occasionally sighted in cold places." This man was very much a loner, quite uncomfortable in one-to-one encounters, and appeared awkward, stiff, and humorless. This personal style would have mattered little if it had affected only himself, but unfortunately he was running a large organization. His detachment from the day-to-day functioning of the company had serious implications for corporate culture and the policy-making process. As his key executives were unsure what was expected of them, they withdrew into their own territories and began to create personal empires. The consequences were lack of cooperation, suboptimization, escalation of internal conflict, and an inconsistent strategy—factors that seriously affected the bottom line.

The Systems Person

For many people with communication difficulties associated with an alexithymic disposition, the technology revolution has been a tremendous facilitator. Problems the individual might have in relating to others are disguised by his or her successful interaction with a machine. The systems person operates in an automatonlike way, clinging to fixed routines and avoiding relationships with people. His or her direction is set by the terminal of a computer, which also seems to furnish all the stimulation such a person requires. Systems-oriented organizations provide a holding environment par excellence for these alexithymics; they can resort to jobs that are thing-oriented, where their attention is focused on abstractions, tasks, ideas, and inanimate objects. Their attachment to machines is a way of coping with the sterility of their inner world. The interview earlier between the psychologist and the executive illustrates the mental state of a person of this type. Although many alexithymics can function extremely well in these circumstances, their often mindless and inflexible pursuit of routines means that curiosity and initiative are missing. They probably will not be sufficiently adaptable to cope with environmental changes, a deficiency that can have devastating repercussions for an organization.

The Social Sensor

> *It's difficult to describe the atmosphere when he was around. He was like the grown-up who switches on the light in the nursery and all the toys, which were magically running around, freeze and turn into toys again. You'd see the effect on people new to the department. They'd start by saying how charming he was then after a while the uneasiness and bewilderment would set in. Getting to know him was like digging a hole in the sand. You keep*

> *hoping you're going to hit something but the further down*
> *you get, the more wet sand you find, and then the sides fall*
> *in and undo all your work. He seemed so interested in*
> *people, always asking questions, always laughing. After a*
> *while you realized the questions were his way of keeping*
> *you at a distance, and he laughed at everything just in case*
> *it was amusing, because he had no natural sense of humor.*

These remarks made by an executive during an interview are indicative of the kind of atmosphere the social sensor creates. The social sensor is in many ways a chameleon, quick to pick up signals from the outside world and adjust his or her behavior accordingly. Predictably, social sensors fit very well in service-oriented industries, where prescribed emotions are the norm. However, despite all their efforts, and notwithstanding this superficial capacity for adjustment, their actions lack conviction. Although they may give an initial impression of complete normality and superadaptability, under this veneer one rapidly uncovers a desperate shallowness and lack of real warmth. Changeability is their only fixed characteristic, resulting in pseudosincerity and pseudoauthenticity. Their superadaptability and compliance have only one goal, which is to avoid having to deal with feelings. What appears as adaptability is really insensitivity to the feelings and reactions of people around them. The mask of extroversion is a disguise for the emptiness of their inner world, which handicaps their creativity and insight.

Jane Lowell (name disguised) was a flight supervisor for an airline, and for many years she had been a model worker—energetic, hardworking, extremely effective, and an example to others. She had always found it easy to tune in to signals given to her by passengers and colleagues. Unfortunately, something strange seemed to be happening to that tuning-in mechanism, and she had started behaving inappropriately at work. There were complaints about her being late, that she failed to respond to customers, and that she had been observed staring into space. When confronted with these criticisms, Lowell explained that she had recently had a lot of physical problems and that the allergies and gastrointestinal disorders she had suffered from all her life had been worse than usual. Feeling that there was more to Jane's problems than physical ill health, the human resource department of the airline suggested that she see a therapist.

During her discussions with the therapist, Lowell began to realize that her body was no longer conforming to her habitual behavior, and that the sensation of physical ill health had begun substituting for emotional experience. The vivid, rebellious sensations of her body made her feel more alive than her prescribed emotional interactions at work. The therapist helped Lowell to become aware of the difficulties she had in recognizing her own feelings. In many respects, the job at the airline had been ideal for her because she responded well to the management of emotions and was able to avoid responsibility for her own feelings. The airline manual and training classes had taught her exactly how to respond in certain situations. But the price she had paid for this sense of security had been high. Lowell realized that, over time, her inner confusion about her own feelings had become more and more critical. It had resulted in a broken engagement and an inability to form new relationships.

She began to examine the part her mother had played in initiating the problems she now had to deal with. Her father had deserted her mother soon after Lowell's birth, and her mother had directed all her nervous energy toward the baby. As a child,

Lowell had never been given much psychic space. Her mother had always seemed able to control Lowell's feelings, thoughts, and fantasies, just as the airline did in later life. The breakdown in her physical health—albeit a primitive, nonverbal option—was Lowell's only way of asserting herself in order to feel alive. Her anorexic behavior in adolescence also now became more understandable, her refusal to eat having been a perverse way of attempting to establish her own identity.

With the help of the therapist, Lowell became increasingly adept at recognizing her own feelings. Like a child learning to name objects, she gradually became able to identify which feeling belonged to what situation. When she became confident about functioning on her own, Lowell decided to leave the airline, considering it wise to find a position where she would not be subject to managed emotions and the risk of reactivating her basic behavior patterns.

Searching for Solutions

The fact that some executives possess or are susceptible to the alexithymic disposition, whether primary or secondary, does not mean that the situation is unchangeable. However, breaking the vicious circle of emotionlessness is not easy, and, unfortunately, there is no quick remedy for the situation. If change is desired, if there is a wish to enliven organizational life, a sustained effort is necessary.

From an institutional perspective, the organization can make structural arrangements that encourage experimentation and participation. In order to foster such behavior, there is also a need for imaginative hiring, training, and development practices, which will in turn avoid the creation of organizations populated by clones. Enough flexibility should be built into organizational systems and culture to allow for continuous adaptations and development.

From an individual perspective, role models become extremely important. The greatest heroes of the business world are those who engage in bold action—Jack Welch, Richard Branson, Carlo de Benedetti, Steven Jobs, Ross Perot—people who have "fire in their belly," who are not afraid of expressing emotion spontaneously. But, all too often, the executive and the "man in the gray flannel suit" become synonymous. Spontaneous emotion is feared as disruptive, and in general the climb to the executive suite is not enhanced by eccentric behavior. Individuals need to be able to see that in their organization there is room for bold moves, leaps of imagination, passion, and vision. Here the individual executive as well as the organization has a responsibility. The individual has to take the initiative and establish preventive measures. On this point, Whyte goes even further and argues for an overtly combative attitude:

> *The organization man is not in the grip of vast social forces about which it is impossible for him to do anything; the options are there, and with wisdom and foresight he can turn the future away from the dehumanized collective that so haunts our thoughts. . . . He must fight The Organization. Not stupidly or selfishly, for the defects of individual self-regard are no more to be venerated than the defects of cooperation. But fight he must, for the demands for his surrender are constant and powerful; and the more he has come to like the life of organization the more difficult does*

he find it to resist these demands, or even to recognize
them. It is wretched dispiriting advice to hold before him
the dream that ideally there need be no conflict between
him and society. There always is; there always must be
[1956, p. 404].

We do not have to go so far as to preach revolution. However, to create effective organizations, an effort must be made to help executives admit their emotions and practice their capacity for self-observation. The tendency of many executives to give in to flight into action without the balance of reflection has to be carefully monitored. Executives have to discover or rediscover the ability to play, to learn how to use humor and how to engage constructively in flights of fantasy. From such abilities vision and true adaptability derive. Executives should be able to confront their feelings and not remain prisoners of a fictitious emotional balance to which they partially contribute. They should not devote their energies to disguising their true self, but show authenticity in action. They should try to overcome infantile fixations and aims. To do so, imaginative experience and fantasy production must be encouraged even if, paradoxically, this imagining sometimes has to be done in a directed way. This task is not just the bailiwick of therapists and consultants. Organizational leaders can play an important role in fostering such practices. More important, leaders can indicate that the expression of emotion is acceptable by showing it themselves. After all, it is passion that gives meaning to organizational life. Organizational leaders should also encourage diversity in emotional expression and not stick just to prescribed routines. Of course, a climate of trust within the organization is essential for these practices to work. Executives have to feel that the expression of emotion in a business context does not have negative career implications, that there is room for contrarian thinking, for critical give and take, and space for imagination. They should keep in mind the words of the poet W. B. Yeats: "By logic and reason we die; by imagination we live."

chapter 5

HUBRIS AND THE FOOL:

humor as a balance to power

The words which would cost a wise man his life
are surprisingly enjoyable when uttered by a clown.
—**Erasmus,** *In Praise of Folly*

Do you think that the things people make fools of themselves
about are any less real than the things they behave sensibly about?
They are more true: they are the only things that are true.
—**George Bernard Shaw,** *Candida*

*i*n Aeschylus's play *The Persians,*
the ghost of Darius, father of Xerxes, king of Persia, laments
the crushing defeat of the Persians at Salamis:

So now for my whole house a staunchless spring of griefs
Is opened; and my son in youthful recklessness,
Not knowing the gods' ways, has been the cause of all.
He hoped to stem that holy stream, the Bosporus,
And bind the Hellespont with fetters like a slave;
He would wrest nature, turn sea into land, manacle
A strait with iron, to make a highway for his troops.
He in his mortal folly thought to overpower

Immortal gods, even Poseidon. Was not this
Some madness that possessed him?

When a storm foiled Xerxes's initial attempt to take his army across the Hellespont, he had the sea whipped as a punishment. But, as Aeschylus narrates, the gods had long ago decreed that the Persians would attain fame only on land. Xerxes's transgression of the will of the gods—an act of hubris—came to a bad end. On September 29, 479 B.C., a naval battle that Xerxes had initiated against the Greeks ended in a massive defeat for the Persians. Mardonius, his brother-in-law and general, was abandoned with his army in Thessaly without a supply line. At a subsequent battle, Mardonius was killed, leading to a withdrawal of the army of occupation.

Not all acts of hubris have such dramatic results—they do not all turn into a cosmic confrontation with the gods. However, a leader's overconfidence, excessive pride, and arrogance can often lead to similarly devastating consequences for an organization. On April 23, 1991, Gerald Ratner, chairman of Britain's largest chain of retail jewelers, made a mildly amusing speech at the annual convention of the Institute of Directors in London. His basic theme was that a company had to be carefully nursed and nurtured through a period of recession. He attributed his company's continuing success to this approach, combined with aggressive marketing, ruthless undercutting of the competition, and close attention to profit margins. Unfortunately he lightened his test with a few jokes about the quality of the jewelry and other gift items that Ratners sold. He said, "We . . . do cut-glass sherry decanters complete with six glasses on a silver-plated tray that your butler can serve you drinks on, all for £4.95. People say: 'How can you sell this for such a low price?' I say, because it is total crap." He had made such jokes many times before, and they had always gone down well with the members of his audience, none of whom had any illusions about the relative importance of price and quality in Ratners product lines. Even more unfortunately, however, the convention and speeches were widely reported in the British press. Many financial analysts, who had been tipping Ratners shares, were displeased with the chairman's caricature of the group. However, their reaction was nothing compared with the scandal and fury unleashed in the British media—especially the tabloid press—the following day.

During the weeks that followed, Ratners managers around the country gamely tried to limit the negative impact of their chairman's injudicious remarks by deliberately playing on them in their publicity and promotions in local outlets. After all, unashamed vulgarity had been the keynote of Ratners success. The chairman had said nothing that his customers were not already well aware of; tastelessness was a feature of both the group's product lines and its promotion techniques. Anyone might have seen that the chairman's personal style bore no relation to the image of his shops. He owned a town house in Mayfair, a riverside home outside London, drove a Mercedes Benz, and was chauffeured in a Bentley. His clothes came from Savile Row; he wore a Cartier watch—and no wedding ring or any other item of jewelery. The customers drawn by the screeching fluorescent banners advertising special offers in every Ratners shop window in every British high street would probably not have resented such a glaring contrast between the company's values and those of its chairman, even had they been aware of it. Ratners gave them what they wanted—cheap and cheerful jewelry at rock-bottom prices. What did arouse people's resentment—and what sent them away from his shops in droves—was that his contempt for his products implied contempt for his customers. Gerald Ratner's decision to get a cheap laugh by holding up to ridicule products on the strength of which he was (at the time) laughing all the way to the bank made the damaging difference. Nobody wanted to see the chairman playing the fool or making a fool of his customers.

Ratner's speech was an act of hubris, of exaggerated self-confidence. He himself recognized the key to his drive to succeed: "Whether we beat the City's forecasts or not doesn't make much difference to my finances but it does make a lot of difference to my ego and my pride. There it is in one word. Ego" (quoted in Bowditch, 1992, p. 23). His egotism, flamboyance, and humor, all of which were essential ingredients for his success, had led him too far. This tactless speech, coupled with the deepening recession and some expensive acquisitions, brought the Ratners group to its knees. In the nine months between April 1991 and January 1992, the value of the group dropped from £460 million to £54 million. In the six months to August 1992 the group had losses of £30.7 million. By that time, Ratner had handed over chairmanship of the group, remaining as chief executive. However, by October 1992 commentators were insisting that recovery of the group would be guaranteed only if Ratner were to surrender all executive interest in the company, and furious shareholders were baying for his blood, calling his £500,000-plus salary "obscene." Finally, on November 25, 1992, Ratner resigned from the company, saying: "The continuing negative press I have attracted leads me to believe that this decision is in the interests of the group and the people working for it" (quoted in Waller, 1992, p. 21). The London *Times* announced his resignation with the headline, "Gerald's little gem was a joke too far" (Waller, 1992, p. 21). More than eighteen months after he gave it, his speech to the Institute of Directors was still being quoted as the cause of his company's dramatic downturn and his own personal failure.

Hubris is a recurring theme in leadership, for the obvious reason that excessive pride and arrogance often accompany power. Given the unequal relationship between leaders and their followers, many leaders take it for granted that they can transgress rules made for lowly mortals. The problem is how to draw their attention to the danger signals of hubris, to prevent them from seeing only what they want to see—a process reinforced by their followers' idealization of them. Is it possible to create a countervailing power against the regressive forces inherent in leader/follower relationships and, if so, how can it be made to work in an organizational setting?

I would like to suggest that an effective instrument for confronting these issues is a modern interpretation of an ancient role, that of the fool. Traditionally, the sage/fool played the role of mediator between leaders and followers, disseminating deep information (that is, going beyond the directly observable) and consciously or unconsciously seeking out the basic significance of events (Geertz, 1973, 1983; Kets de Vries and Miller, 1987). By looking at organizational roles in this way, we can see that Ratner's mistake was to step out of role; whether he liked it or not, he was cast as the wise man and should have resisted the temptation to play the clown. He was probably the only man in

Britain who could *not* get away with calling Ratners products "total crap." Erasmus's aphorism (quoted at the beginning of this chapter) is more than a bon mot. *In Praise of Folly* examines the traditional relationship between the fool and the leader and the special value of this relationship in limiting the effects of hubris.

The Dangers of Hubris

Hubris is a predictable offshoot of uncontrolled narcissism. Narcissism, which is a key force behind the desire for leadership and power, frequently becomes pronounced once leadership and power are attained. We see then, as Freud noted, a leader who "love[s] no one else, . . . of a masterful nature, absolutely narcissistic, self-confident and independent" ([1921] 1953c, pp. 123–124). Such leaders, who may easily retreat into a world of their own, can be myopic, self-opinionated, and not given to soliciting or accepting advice from others. In many instances they create their own reality and remain resolutely blind to the possible negative consequences of doing so. As I suggested earlier, the situation can be further aggravated by the relationship between leader and followers, which is not always of a rational nature. At times a kind of mutual regression occurs and gives rise to behavior that is inappropriate to the circumstances. Transferential patterns, whereby a leader is idealized and mirrored by followers, seem to be at the heart of these regressive processes, during which the real person and reality are lost.

It is a rare individual who can face reality without becoming caught up in the kinds of primitive defense processes that lead to hubris. Usually, people may become victims of folie à deux, or group think (Kets de Vries, 1989; Janis and Mann, 1977), and engage in irrational decision making. As in therapeutic situations, help may be required in identifying the distortions of reality.

The Role of the Fool

Historically, the person who assumed such a stabilizing role in relation to the leader, usually an emperor or king, was the fool. I am not, of course, using the term in the sense of a person who is stupid and lacking in judgment—quite the reverse—but in the sense of the fool's transformational role as truthsayer. With this relationship, the destinies of the leader and fool become intricately bound in a common fate. The fool creates a certain emotional ambiance and through various means reminds the leader of the transience of power. He becomes the guardian of reality and, in a paradoxical way, prevents the pursuit of foolish action. It is interesting to note that the French satirist Rabelais gave Triboulet, the famous fool at the court of Francis I, the name *morosophe* (Lever, 1983, p. 181), an intriguing combination of words: in Greek, *moros* means fool, while *sophos* means wise or clever.

Fools are widely recognized as a social type. We have all encountered them and at times may have played the fool ourselves. Moreover, we are also familiar with fools from anthropology, myth, folklore, literature, and drama under many different names—tricksters, jesters, buffoons, comics, Harlequins, and Pierrots, for example. Elaborate anthropological descriptions of the ritual fool can be found in studies of African, Asian, Oceanic, North American, Mesoamerican, and South

American communities (Steward, 1931; Bunzel, 1932; Charles, 1945; Radin, [1956] 1969; Makarius, 1969, 1970, 1973). The trickster is endowed with uncanny powers of insight and prophecy. He (the fool is usually a male figure) is both underdog and cult hero, a mirror to people, a jester who produces order out of chaos by connecting the unexplainable to the familiar. Jung describes the trickster as "a primitive 'cosmic' being of divine-animal nature, on the one hand superior to man because of his superhuman qualities, and on the other hand inferior to him because of his unreason and unconsciousness" ([1959] 1969, p. 144). When we compare the role of this mythic creature in different cultures, we see how the trickster becomes a symbol of the human condition, parodying human drives, needs, and weaknesses, combining cunning with stupidity, and being simultaneously funny and frightening. Anthropological research suggests that the trickster is a figure onto whom we can project our own foibles, ideals, and fears, and as such plays an important role in many societies. Welsford goes so far as to call the fool an educator, "for he draws out the latent folly in his audience" (1935, p. 28). By setting a negative example, the fool reinforces true values and valid actions.

Quite apart from the fool's ethnographic incidence, the role has been institutionalized in the professions of clown, buffoon, and court jester (Swain, 1932; Welsford, 1935; Klapp, 1972; Lever, 1983). The jester is privileged in that, under the guise of madness or stupidity (which suggest harmlessness), he can iterate the otherwise unspeakable. He employs all sorts of strategies to convey his message, including clumsiness, exaggeration, absent-mindedness, concealment, pantomime, and botched acts (Bergson, 1928). He has been called a living caricature (Kris,

1938). Certainly, in relation to the king, the jester's traditional props of cap-and-bells and bladder-on-a-stick are an unsubtle mockery of the ruler's crown and scepter. Above all, the jester knows how to apply humor, which serves him as both a weapon and a shield:

> *Jaques:* Is not this a rare fellow, my lord? He's as good at any thing, and yet a fool!

> *Duke:* He uses his folly like a stalking-horse, and under the presentation of that he shoots his wit [Shakespeare, *As You Like It*, act 5, scene 4].

Perhaps the most famous illustration of the transformational role of the fool is that provided by the Fool in Shakespeare's tragedy *King Lear*. Although in appearance only a half-witted boy, he is the sole person close to the king who has the wisdom and courage to recognize and speak the truth. It is important, when considering the figures of fools in drama, not to lose sight of the usefulness of such an ambivalent figure to the dramatist. The fool can be exploited endlessly to explicate the emotional dynamics of the action. The Fool in *King Lear* is a complex and unique figure, whose dramatic function is of great importance. As Muir explains: "He provides not so much comic relief as a safety valve for the audience. Lear's conduct is absurd, if judged critically; and the representation of madness is apt to arouse more laughter than sympathy. The Fool was therefore inserted to draw the laughs of the audience, and to preserve Lear's sublimity" (1952, p. xiv).

I would like to suggest that the power of the leader needs the folly of the fool. The interaction of the two keeps each—and the organization—in psychological equilibrium. The impossibility of the two roles being played by the same person is demonstrated by Ratner's disastrous faux pas. He tried—albeit briefly—to play the fool to his own king. As a result he drew laughter on himself and destroyed his own sublimity (or standing as leader) and with it the credibility of his organization. The duality of the king/fool relationship emphasizes the Janus-faced nature of power. The sage/fool is often the only person who can protect the king from hubris. In the context of more general leadership pathology, the fool has an important role to play. By demonstrating the foolishness of decisions made because of impaired vision, the fool can help the leader to maintain a firm reality base.

The Use of Humor

It would not be too much to claim that humor is of infinite use in an organization and has an enormous amount to contribute to its health and vitality. Humor is a form of metacommunication (Bateson, 1953)—that is, more is communicated through it than is immediately apparent. Humor provides a gentle way of dealing with conflicts, preventing the sudden explosion of tension. It can be a formidable weapon against those who, in other circumstances, would refuse to recognize or accept the truth. Humor humbles; it helps to foster a sense of proportion and to prevent our taking ourselves too seriously. It is instrumental in promoting insight and as such is an instrument for change. It can also operate as a sort of safety valve, controlling the potentially destructive aspects of leadership.

Humor is a good means of highlighting the signs of hubris. It is also a covert way of approaching taboo subjects. Humor can be used to change a strained situation into a pleasant one. Shared laughter contributes to group cohesiveness and enhances cordiality (Roy, 1960; Duncan, 1982). It cuts the distance between leader and led. In addition, humor can also be viewed as a signifier of mental health: "When I see a patient whom I am really concerned about and wonder if there is much hidden paranoia, I always feel reassured when I see a glimpse of the capacity for humor, enough security in the self to appreciate the relativity of the self and the recognition of other selves" (Kohut, 1985, p. 239). According to the psychiatrist George E. Vaillant, "Humor is one of the truly elegant defenses in the human repertoire. Few would deny that the capacity for humor, like hope, is one of mankind's most potent antidotes for the woes of Pandora's box" (1977, p. 116).

With their use of humor, fools can do the otherwise unthinkable, trespassing on forbidden territory and satirizing both leaders and followers. They provide an outlet for the most basic antisocial feelings and, by creating absurd situations, articulate the fears and anxieties of others. Their targets, or audience, experience a sense of relief through the fools' vicarious gratification of unconscious wishes. The self-depreciation that accompanies their transgression of taboos makes their actions less threatening and more easily accepted. It is difficult to hold fools responsible for their actions, as fools seem to have some protective immunity. Something said in jest does not carry the same weight as it does in ordinary communication. Consequently, the fool can take greater risks in communicating a message.

Their behavior and actions suggest that fools know, consciously or unconsciously, the power of the underdog. They know that humorous self-depreciation makes other people feel better. The antics of fools make it possible for us to unload our feelings of inferiority onto them and, by doing so, feel virtuous in comparison with such misfits. However, despite the unique potency of humor as a device that is weapon and protection at the same time, fools are not impregnable. They constantly run the risk of turning into a scapegoat, of representing an evil or malignant force that has to be expelled. Such danger has always been an occupational hazard for a fool.

The anthropologist A. R. Radcliffe-Brown sees joking relationships as a way of managing potential conflicts in society: "The joking relationship is a peculiar combination of friendliness and antagonism. The behavior is such that in any other social context it would express and arouse hostility, but it is not meant seriously and must not be taken seriously. There is a pretense of hostility and a real friendliness. To put it another way, the relationship is one of permitted disrespect" (1952, p. 90). Freud ([1905] 1953f) came to a similar conclusion. He noticed that people used humor as a socially acceptable way of releasing anxiety-provoking wishes of an aggressive and sexual nature. In particular, humor allows for the expression of aggressive and vengeful feelings that otherwise would not be tolerated (Levine, 1961). Laughter can mask many other emotions as well, such as sadness, despair, fear, regret, triumph, and hate.

Freud also wrote that "humor is not resigned; it is rebellious" ([1927] 1953d, p. 103). Joking is frequently used as a way of getting back at figures of authority. The fool is an anarchist, using humor to make the breaking of rules and regulations less objectionable than it would otherwise be (Goffman, 1967). However, this is a tame, covert rebellion, a form of nonviolent resistance (Bergler, 1937). Paradoxically, given its rebellious origins, humor can also become a safety valve, an instrument of social control and regulation (Levine, 1961; Berlyne, 1964). One way of looking at the behavior of fools is that they are actually engaged in setting the limits of the permissible despite their ridicule of the established order. The break from day-to-day conventionality that their behavior implies is only temporary. As the social scientists Howard Pollio and John Edgerly indicate in their research on humor, "In this role of moralist-in-reverse the fool acts as a control mechanism stressing what he violates by emphasizing what is beyond him. To call a non-fool, *fool*, is to put social pressure on that individual to conform to a social value" (1976, p. 216, emphasis added).

The Organizational Fool

If we accept that the fool has an indispensable part to play in the healthy functioning of social life, we have to ask whether that role can be incorporated into organizational life, which represents an intensive microcosm of human society. In organizational life there are many ways to create checks and balances as a form of protection against the abuse of power. These checks can be built into the organizational infrastructure, in the form of rules and regulations. Additionally, power can be distributed among a number of internal and external constituencies. However, despite the various structural safeguards that may be adopted, the fact is that most organizations are anything but democratic. Many important decisions are made in secret by a few people. Help is needed to prevent the abuse of power in organizations and to limit the loss of reality-based decision making. There is a part to be played by a courageous individual who is willing to challenge the leader and give him or her a different perspective, free from the distortions of sycophancy. I like to call this person the organizational fool; however, the protection for this person needs to be more subtle than the fool's traditional cap, bells, and bladder-on-a-stick, and the integration of the modern-day fool into organizational life is more problematic.

Just as the sage/fool or truthsayer was playing with fire when telling the king unpleasant truths, it is risky to point out hidden agendas within a organization (Malone, 1980). It is notoriously difficult to establish open communication within organizations, even where intentions are good. More often than not, company structure is actively hostile to such a process and mere lip service is paid to the principle. Many managers and leaders operate in splendid isolation and are more than content to do so; a great deal of their energy is devoted to protecting the autonomy of their patch. This way of operating generates an atmosphere of caution and playing-safe within the organization. Even if open communication is genuinely encouraged—a relatively rare occurrence—human nature can prove surprisingly resistant to it. Half the world expects to be told what to do, and the other half to do the telling. The larger the organization, the bigger the problem.

It is a truism that power—the ability to do great harm or great good—leads to the suspension of moral values. Power frequently substitutes for trust in business relationships, whether between individuals within an organization or between one organization and others it deals with. And in the absence of trust, problems that remain untreated accumulate. When they surface, it is usually explosively, loaded with emotionally charged material.

One manifestation of this effect is whistle-blowing.

When I realized what was happening, I was furious. It wasn't illegal, it wasn't criminal, it was . . . irresponsible. Every day the papers wrote about cutbacks in funding [the service], nearly every day I got reminders about cost saving, and here were resources being mismanaged and squandered so obviously it was beyond belief. I went to my superiors but it was like talking to a brick wall. So I went to the papers myself. I didn't have much to lose, I was down for early retirement, but I did it anonymously anyway. All hell was let loose, somehow they found out who I was, I had the press and TV outside my house, and at work the atmosphere was unbearable. And in the end nothing happened. It was a five-minute wonder for the press. It all got lost in the bureaucratic mess of the service [public service worker, Great Britain].

Whistle-blowing is always more or less disastrous for both the individual and the organization. When communication is blocked within an organization, or when an individual feels isolated and without support, it is tempting to turn to outside entities, such as the media, to air grievances. It is virtually impossible for the individual to escape the resulting fallout and hostility from all sides, especially as an organization exposed in this manner is hardly likely to provide the support and protection that the whistle-blower needs—the lack of which probably precipitated the action in the first place. The painful irony for whistle-blowers is that their personal integrity and trustworthiness, which originally motivated their actions, are put into doubt, and they frequently end up being blamed for the very things they exposed. This is the classic reaction of killing the messenger who brings bad news. Whistle-blowers are fools working without their protective clothing.

Freud struggled with the issues of trust and communication from the early days of his research and commented on them in his paper " 'Wild' Psycho-analysis." He felt that informing another person of unconscious material would work only if two conditions were fulfilled:

> *First, the patient must, through preparation, himself have reached the neighborhood of what he has repressed, and secondly, he must have formed a sufficient attachment (transference) to the physician for his emotional relationships to him to make . . . flight impossible.*
>
> *Only when these conditions have been fulfilled is it possible to recognize and to master the resistances which have led to repression and the ignorance. Psychoanalytic intervention, therefore, absolutely requires a fairly long period of contact with the patient. Attempts to "rush" him at first consultation, by brusquely telling him the secrets which have been discovered by the physician, are technically objectionable ([1910] 1953g, p. 226).*

As Freud indicates, in order to ease the surfacing of emotionally charged material, a working alliance must first be established between the two parties in question. To form this alliance, a certain amount of trust is needed. Freud realized that the task of building such a relationship requires considerable delicacy. Doses of insight have to be well-timed and carefully measured (Kets de Vries and Miller, 1984). If this control is not established, a runaway situation may develop, and the truthsayer may turn into the sorcerer's apprentice, unable to stem the flood released. The sage/fool must realize that there are limits to the amount of conflict-ridden material a leader (or anyone) can accept at any given time. Here the fool does not usually have the advantage of the psychotherapist in having frequent, formally arranged encounters and a well-established bond. In an organizational setting the encounters are often haphazard.

Fortunately, as I indicated earlier, humor plays an important role in relieving tension when a point has to be made about a sensitive issue: humor facilitates the reception of such information. It short-circuits resistance and improves the readiness of people to hear what must be done to keep the organization on track. A good example of the role played by a sage/fool in one particular form of organizational life is found in Jaroslav Hasek's famous novel *The Good Soldier Svejk*, which describes the misadventures of a seemingly idiotic hero and satirizes the decaying Austro-Hungarian empire and its war machine. In a certain sense, Svejk represents anybody who finds himself trapped in the cogs of bureaucracy. His idiocy is really a cloak for his wit and wisdom. He is a careful observer of humanity, and his penetrating commentary makes others realize the absurdity of their actions. Svejk is an excellent example of the sage/fool. Through double-talk and the literal execution of orders, he demonstrates the foolishness of many rules and regulations. His behavior and actions force us to rethink the rationale behind our own conduct. He is the perfect antidote to hubris.

But would Svejk find a place in a business organization and, if so, what would his staying powers be? This last is a crucial question. The organizational fool takes definite risks in dealing with highly sensitive material. Telling the truth can be threatening to career advancement, and whistle-blowing usually spells a bad end for the individual who initiates the process. For these reasons, it is difficult for an insider to take on the role. However, fools can be found in organizations, and they can be extremely effective in influencing leadership. Occasionally a trusted senior executive plays the part, perhaps because this role has evolved naturally as a function of the job. Some organizations have institutionalized positions, such as internal consultants, or a kind of ombudsman (following the Scandinavian tradition) or a senior executive without portfolio. With certain skills of dramatization, even a less senior manager may occasionally become a spokesperson. In some organizations, it may be preferable to have someone at a less elevated level—an Everyman or Svejk—playing the part.

Let us take an example. In one company in the automobile-supply business, the role of the fool was played by the vice president for manufacturing and operations. A self-made man who had risen in the company through the production route, he was intimately familiar with the internal processes of the organization. He was extremely effective in his job and highly respected for his pragmatism. Given his background and the fact that the company was market-driven, he had risen as far as he could. This position did not seem to bother him, however, as he obviously liked it. Because he did not pose a threat to the other executives—power games were the least of his concerns—his advice was eagerly sought. Although the company had a director of human resources, this man informally played an important role in that area.

When the CEO retired, a successor was appointed from within the conglomerate of which the company formed a part. The new CEO was not knowledgeable about the company or the industry, having worked in a different sector. He was abrasive when dealing with subordinates, quick to cut them off or silence them with sarcastic remarks when things were not exactly to his liking. The atmosphere within the company became tense and grew worse when two long-serving directors were dismissed after a heated executive meeting. The company's executives were at a loss to know how to deal with the new CEO. Because of his difficult temperament, they were reluctant to oppose him even when they felt he was making decisions that were not in the best interests of the company.

At this point the vice president for manufacturing and operations began to play an increasingly visible role at executive meetings. In a humorous way—without being aggressive or derogatory—he was able to defuse the emotionally charged atmosphere and simultaneously communicate to the CEO the not-publicly-expressed consensus of the group. His self-effacing and humorous style had a calming effect on the CEO, who, it seems, had in part been acting as he had because of his own anxiety about how to tackle his job. Under the influence of the vice president, executive meetings became more of a give-and-take. Gradually, the other executives grew sufficiently courageous to express their own opinions freely. When aspects of the CEO's antagonistic style reemerged, the vice president was quick to neutralize the situation, and the openness of exchange was maintained.

Generally speaking, however, it is easier for an outsider to take on this sort of role. It is frequently assumed by a consultant, for example, although in the normal course of events it is not a function for which a consultant is specifically employed. Often both parties are unaware that the consultant is acting the part and that the organization is being firmly tied to reality because the consultant is playing that role. (Occasionally, senior executives do realize how important a corporate jester can be. I have been present at meetings where short satirical sketches were effectively used to relay difficult messages to top management. I have seen similar role-playing activities used elsewhere in the company in a structured or in a spontaneous way. In general, these activities are directed toward middle management rather than top executives, and their effectiveness is correspondingly limited.)

Quite frequently consultants realize that the real problem in an organization is different from the one originally defined. The gap between what clients say they want and what they really need can be huge. Because executives are often reluctant to raise and confront the real issues, it is the consultant's responsibility to search beyond the symptoms and bring difficult contributing factors into the open. If consultants play the fool with tact and discretion, they can be an important catalyst for insight and change.

The consequences of falling into "wild analysis" tend to be less dramatic with a consultant playing the fool than with an insider doing so. The worst that can happen when the feedback becomes too disturbing is a prematurely terminated consultancy. In many ways, the role of the external adviser and that of the fool seem to be made for each other. By playing dumb and asking deliberately naive questions, the consultant can further the understanding of a particular organizational problem and become an agent for change. Humor can be invaluable here, particularly when suggesting options and making recommendations.

In one organization, an external consultant was brought in to rationalize the workflow in the design department. His suggestions proved to be highly effective and produced a burst of activity throughout the organization. Because of his success, the consultant was asked to help design and implement a new performance-appraisal system. The CEO, normally rather an aloof individual, whom others found difficult to approach, very much appreciated the work of the consultant and began to take him into his confidence. Because the CEO was not completely satisfied with the way executive meetings operated, he asked the consultant to sit in on some of the sessions and recommend ways of improving the quality of decision making. The consultant quickly realized that the CEO's own awkwardness stifled the free flow of information and creative ideas and was responsible for the painfully stilted discussions that took place. Changes were needed if the sessions were to become more productive. As his attendance at meetings continued, the consultant began to ask pseudonaive questions about the different issues under discussion, and his humor lightened the atmosphere. His interventions helped to break the ice, while simultaneously emphasizing important points. Gradually, all the executives began to relax and the discussions became much more creative than they had been, with people listening to one another and building on each other's ideas.

Like so much else in organizational life, however, the

successful establishment of this kind of relationship and culture depends very much on enlightened management and leadership. Where the leader is determined to make communication processes work and recognizes the pitfalls involved in loss of trust, the problems are greatly eased. One person who makes these issues a principle of his leadership is the French financier, entrepreneur, and politician Bernard Tapie. In his autobiography, *Gagner* (*Winning*), he writes:

> *Even the most intelligent and shrewd of leaders surround themselves with people who surrender their individuality and spirit of opposition when face to face with their boss. . . . They say nothing, even when they see the leader leading the company astray, because they don't dare to. . . . A great leader will of his own volition institute a culture of deliberate irresponsibility. For me, frank discussion and what I call creative tension are absolutely fundamental. For this reason I have a network of friends whom I consult just as much as I consult my team. They are journalists, businessmen, a mixture of very different people who are completely independent of me, who aren't my employees, and who will tell me where to get off—and that's crucial. If you haven't got people around who'll tell you when to take a running jump, you're not a proper boss. . . .*
>
> *In order to choose the right sort of people to have around, the sort who also want to be "winners," you have to know yourself, to be open to contradictory opinions, to be able to work out where your own strengths and weaknesses lie [1986, pp. 126–127].*

These various examples illustrate how the sage/fool, whether personified as an individual or institutionalized as a team, can act as a counterweight to the person in power. As a result, a kind of executive constellation is formed that can be highly effective in preventing organizational pathology (Hodgson, Levinson, and Zaleznik, 1965). Through humor and frank communication, the "fool" and the "king" engage in a form of deep play that deals with fundamental issues of human nature, such as control, rivalry, passivity, and activity. If humor is controlled and not allowed to become damaging or overaggressive, it can contribute to group cohesion and an atmosphere of trust. It provides a method of working through destructive fantasies and can have a soothing effect that may eventually redirect an organization toward reality issues.

Unfortunately, in studying organizations we usually focus on leaders and seldom turn our attention to the roles of subordinates. However, there is an intricate link between the two: leaders need followers, the king needs his fool, and vice versa. We must not forget that in spite of the rationality that supposedly pervades organizations, the truth of the matter is often quite different. A thin line divides the forces of reality and wishful thinking. When the boundaries fade, the consequences can be devastating for effective organizational functioning. This is precisely where the organizational fool can play a crucial role. George Bernard Shaw once said that "every despot must have one disloyal subject to keep him sane." That is the function of the fool. Within an organization, someone playing the fool can help keep it on track, maintain its grip on reality, and, most important of all, check the destructive force of hubris.

chapter 6

THE IMPOSTOR SYNDROME

*Hard to say exactly what the manner was, any more
than to hint it was a sort of magical; in a benign way,
not wholly unlike the manner, fables or otherwise,
of certain creatures in nature, which have
the power of persuasive fascination—
the power of holding another creature
by the button of the eye, as it were, despite the serious
disinclination, and, indeed, earnest protest, of the victim.*
—Herman Melville, *The Confidence Man*

*I am well aware that an addiction to silk underwear
does not necessarily imply that one's feet are dirty.
None the less, style, like sheer silk,
too often hides eczema.*
—Albert Camus, *The Fall*

*t*hroughout history, impostors
have fascinated the public. People leading fraudulent lives or
engaging in fraudulent activities have always held a fatal attraction. One reason for their popularity may be the element of
recognition—it often seems as if impostors show us something
about ourselves that we may prefer not to see under normal

circumstances. And to some extent, considering the differences between the ways we present our public and our private self, we are all impostors—we all play roles (Goffman, 1971). Displaying a facade and misleading our audience are part and parcel of everyday life. However, this is not a sufficient explanation for the ease with which impostors can make fools of their audience in situations of true imposture. Frequently, the audience is all too willing to be imposed on.

The term *impostor* has two connotations that are often concurrent. An impostor can be someone who deceives, swindles, or cheats. It can also be someone who assumes a false character and passes himself or herself off as something other than he or she really is. We find situations in which the two roles are combined, when someone takes on a false identity in order to swindle others. But we also encounter individuals who pass themselves off as someone else without obtaining any visible benefits from doing so. The situation in which the impostor benefits is the more common; nevertheless, financial gain should probably be regarded as a means to an end rather than the principal reason for the impostor's actions, even in these cases. Psychological gratification often seems to be much more important than the material advantages that can be won by imposture.

Of the many examples of imposture we could choose, perhaps none is more staggeringly audacious than the career of Ferdinand Waldo Demara, alias The Great Impostor (Crichton, 1959). Reading his life story, we can only marvel at the ease with which this man assumed an amazing variety of identities. Demara managed to pass himself off as a Trappist monk, a doctor of psychology and dean of the school of philosophy at a small college in Pennsylvania, a law student, a zoology graduate, a cancer researcher and teacher at a junior college in Maine, a surgeon-lieutenant in the Royal Canadian Navy (actually performing major surgery—successfully—at sea), an assistant warden of a Texas prison, and a schoolteacher.

A memorable example of imposture in business is that of Anthony De Angelis, whose manipulation of millions of gallons of nonexistent salad oil sent two Wall Street brokerage houses into bankruptcy, caused the failure of a subsidiary of the American Express Company and led to plummeting futures prices on commodity markets in New York and Chicago (Miller, 1965). Although certainly motivated by financial gain, De Angelis also created a remarkable world of make-believe to satisfy his need for recognition. He outsmarted dozens of the world's shrewdest bankers, brokers, and businessmen. While he played his con game, however, nobody stopped to wonder how he could make money by selling salad oil at such impossibly low prices. Instead, he continually sweet-talked financiers into lending him more money for the next deal. The wish to believe, fueled by greed, made even the most astute businessman suspend reality and disbelief. Eventually, the financiers were holding papers for astounding quantities of salad oil, more than could be accounted for according to government reports on existing stocks. But still nobody was alarmed. Only after eight years of operation did the bubble burst and the authorities discover that De Angelis's salad-oil tanks were empty.

There is even a rather unusual psychiatric classification of imposture, the Münchhausen syndrome, a condition named after the fictional eighteenth-century German baron and soldier-adventurer who is the hero of many tall tales (Lehmann, 1975; Swanson, 1981). The condition is characterized by repeated fabrication of clinically convincing symptoms and a false medical and social history. The wish of people suffering from this syndrome is to be given surgical or other forms of treatment for a nonpsychiatric medical illness.

When we view the lives of people like Demara and De Angelis with hindsight, it often seems incomprehensible that anyone could have fallen for their tricks. While the confidence game is being played, however, the impostor, like the Pied Piper of Hamelin, seems to weave a magic spell, and people are only too ready to follow. Impostors seem to be able to awaken otherwise dormant tendencies within us by which we can be carried away, blinded to reality. Moreover, imposture may well be a far more widespread phenomenon than we think. Clinical investigation suggests that it is a characteristic with a range running from feeling like a fraud to being actively involved in fraudulent activities. It is certainly difficult to think of a piece of drama or fiction in which the action is not motivated largely by imposture or unmasking—and it is not stretching the point too far to say that these preoccupations make up a large percentage of hard daily news.

So what makes someone an impostor? What do impostors want? What motivates them? Why are they so fascinating? Why are they so self-destructive (after all, they are by and large found out)? Is there an element of the impostor in all of us? What are the particular problems raised by imposturous behavior in organizational life?

The Psychodynamics of Imposture

The earliest known clinical paper on the impostor was written by Karl Abraham ([1925] 1955). As an army doctor, Abraham was asked by a military court to investigate a conscript facing court martial. He wrote in his case history how impressed he was by the conscript's ability to gain the trust of others (including his jailers) and then to betray their confidence immediately through deception. Abraham was particularly struck by the conscript's "genius for phantastic story telling" and his "uncontrollable desire for aggrandizement" (p. 294). In explanation, Abraham suggested that because this particular individual "felt himself unloved in his childhood, he had an inner urge to show himself 'lovable' to everybody . . . [and then] to prove to himself and to show them soon afterward how unworthy he was of such feeling" (p. 300). Abraham also pointed to the conscript's longing for rich parents, symptomatic of what is called in clinical literature the "family romance"—the perpetuation of a relatively common childhood fantasy (particularly after having been punished) that one's parents are not the real ones and that one is really of noble or royal descent. In this way, one's real parents are viewed as frauds. The fantasy that somewhere there must be some other, better, more understanding parents lingers on. This feeling is triggered by the parents' failure to respond to the child's need for recognition and independence. Family-romance fantasies can be regarded as forms of compensatory narcissistic self-enhancement, attempts to regulate self-esteem (Kaplan, 1974). These fantasies contribute to the development of a "personal myth" (Kris, 1975), a combination of early memories and fantasies, which serves as an organizer of later experience. Abraham also commented on the strong self-defeating streak in the conscript's behavior, in that "he never showed much aptitude for eluding the arm of the law" (p. 292).

In her discussion of impostors in 1955, Deutsch inferred

that impostors assume the identities of others "not because they themselves lack the ability for achievement, but because they have to hide under a strange name to materialize a more or less reality adapted fantasy" ([1955] 1965a, p. 332). She suggested that "the ego of the impostor, as expressed in his own true name, is devaluated, guilt-laden" (p. 332). No wonder that such a person feels compelled to function under other, more glorious covers more in line with his or her conception of how he or she really wishes to be. From her case example, Deutsch surmised that the unusual behavior of the impostor is caused by the emotional "overfeeding" of the child by the mother, who smothers her offspring with her affections. The father's behavior may aggravate the situation, as he may overburden the child by making him or her the recipient of his own unfulfilled desires. Deutsch also considered individuals who, having achieved success, are troubled by the feeling that they are impostors. Of her patient, she commented that "the more effectively [he] functioned in reality, the more anxiety he developed. . . . He felt like an impostor in his new role, that of doing honest work" (p. 333).

Greenacre ([1958] 1971a, [1958] 1971b) postulated three basic sets of symptoms in cases of imposture: "First, the dominant and dynamically active family romance; second, the intense and circumscribed disturbance of the sense of identity, a kind of infarction in the sense of reality; third, a malformation of the superego involving both conscience and ideals" (1971b, p. 96). She commented on the apparent need of impostors for self-betrayal, having been struck by a marked discrepancy in their abilities: "skill and persuasiveness are combined with utter foolishness and stupidity" (1971b, p. 97). Greenacre recognized the necessity of the audience's reaction to help the impostor establish a realistic sense of self. She traced the genesis of this behavior to a family in which the parents are at odds with each other and the child is treated with extreme possessiveness by the mother and used as an item of exhibitionistic display. At the same time the mother may downgrade the father as being ineffective and disappointing. Greenacre suggested that there was, in these cases, a serious imbalance in the oedipal situation, with the child (in the case of a male impostor) seemingly superseding the father in the family. She argued that the child is forced into an adult role prematurely. In order to maintain this position, and gain and continue to capture the admiration of grownups, a child will develop astounding talents in mimicry, most noticeably the ability to imitate adult behavior. Unfortunately, the price of such a developmental track is often the lack of a well-formed separate self and a poor sense of identity and reality.

Impostors carry this gift for mimicry into adulthood, becoming highly skilled in colluding with their audience in order to create an ambiance of make-believe and appear more grandiose than they are. The family romance also takes on an adult form, with fantasies of self-aggrandizement continuing to play an important part in the impostor's life. The behavior of impostors also has an element of what of sometimes called *pseudologica phantastica* (Fenichel, 1954; Deutsch, 1965b), when the elaborate lies the impostor makes up to impress an audience act as screen memories, simultaneously revealing and concealing events that have really happened. In his zeal, the impostor may be convinced of their truth. *Pseudologica phantastica* and pathological lying differ importantly from the normal fantasies of daydreaming because reality testing is suspended long enough to allow the impostor to act out his or her fantasies, if only to convince the audience. Fabrication of a new "truth" is also a way of covering up painful psychological material containing grains of historical truth (Weinshel, 1979; Spence, 1982; Blum, 1983). In this way, lies are a form of self-protection, as they give the impostor control over threatening inner conflict.

It is not a particularly large step from this point to the loss of the capacity to differentiate between fantasy and reality—the stage at which impostors begin to believe the myth they have created about themselves. The smallness of this step is probably explained by the fact that impostors often feel better when they assume the identity of someone else. They seem to reject and devalue their own identity, despite their awareness of their own genuine gifts and talents. In fact, they frequently make use of these talents to develop their imposturous behavior. One of the most common ways in which they use their talents is in their manipulation of language—their power with words and their ability to listen. Like many writers of fiction, they understand how to fabricate illusions and how to make these illusions convincing. Langer (1953) describes how audiences reveled in medieval troubadours' descriptions of scenes and demanded ever greater elaboration and detail, as if they were building up a three-dimensional painting. Impostors, with their capacity for empathetic response and their sensitivity to cues from their audience, also weave the audience's desires into their own myth, creating an increasingly credible tapestry of illusion.

Someone in whom the crisis of identity, the power of language, and the skill of myth making met and combined with both creative and tragic results was the eighteenth-century English poet Thomas Chatterton. Chatterton was the posthumous son of a Bristol schoolmaster and was raised by his mother and sister. He was precocious and brilliant and by the time he was sixteen had already written the poems on which his reputation rests. However, he passed the poems off as medieval manuscripts that he had found in an old chest, producing further faked documents to back up his discovery. When his fraud was exposed, Chatterton fled to London, where, in misery and poverty, he took his own life at the age of seventeen. What were Chatterton's poems about?

> *Chatterton [fabricated] in his writings an imaginatively conceived family romance, which even included a perfected medieval city of Bristol, changing it to a radiant fifteenth-century metropolis whose cultural center was the very church in which generations of Chattertons had been the sextons. Written at what must often have been white heat, in an ostensible Middle English which was really his own neologistic invention, he idealized and fictionalized an actual fifteenth-century Bristol merchant and mayor into a saintlike philanthropist, warrior, and humanitarian, a man of the world who lived an exemplary religious life and who commissioned a priest-poet, Rowley, to write the chronicles and to eulogize the city's history. The evidence suggests that Rowley was a perfected projection of Chatterton himself, while the saintly merchant, Canynge, was his father [Olinick, 1988, p. 674].*

The writer of fiction can be said to be continually engaging in a form of harmless imposture, requiring the willing collusion of his readers in his fabrications. Chatterton pushed this mutual, consenting deception over the moral boundary between fiction and fraud to satisfy some aspect of his own injured narcissism. Deprived of a father-figure, perhaps forced into a role he felt unable to sustain by the expectations of his mother and sister, unsure of his own identity, deprecating and disguising his own talents, Chatterton fabricated and externalized a personal romance of extraordinary potency. His reputation and verse have survived his exposure and humiliation; his tragic death has inspired other poets and artists. Beyond his appeal to the romantic imagination, the kernel of real genius in his writing was recognized by many. William Wordsworth described him as "the marvellous Boy," while John Keats declared him "the purest writer in the English language."

Symbolically, impostors seem to take on the role of the archaic, all-caring mother, satisfying oceanic longings, gratifying an almost-forgotten but never really relinquished childhood desire for total attention. To their audience, impostors represent someone who understands all their needs, can express their deepest desires, and will take care of them. To the impostor, the greediness of the audience for more of the same is a constant stimulus. The fantasy world of the audience, once the impostor has successfully penetrated it, contains infinite demands. In this way, impostor and audience are linked by a compatibility of interests in an unconscious conspiracy; as the actor W. C. Fields once said, "You can't cheat an honest man." The audience is kept happy by the expectation that it will have its demands met, while the impostor needs the audience to counteract an inner sense of emptiness and reaffirm some kind of identity. Of course, the audience is most susceptible in times of crisis and upheaval, when imposture can occur on a grand scale, given either an acknowledged or an unspoken need for a savior. In the context of societal turmoil there has been one outstanding example of a way of acting which contains imposturous elements, this time seen in a political context.

> *One of the secrets of his mastery over a great audience was his instinctive sensitivity to the mood of a crowd, a flair for divining the hidden passions, resentments and longings in their minds. . . .*
>
> *One of his most bitter critics [Hanfstängl, 1957] . . . wrote:*
>
> *[He] responds to the vibrations of the human heart with the delicacy of a seismograph, or perhaps of a wireless receiving set, enabling him, with a certainty with which no conscious gift could endow him, to act as a loudspeaker proclaiming the most secret desires, the least admissible instincts, the sufferings, and personal revolts of a whole nation. . . . His uncanny intuition . . . infallibly diagnoses the ills from which his audience is suffering. . . . [He] enters a hall. He sniffs the air. For a minute he gropes, feels his way, senses the atmosphere. Suddenly he bursts forth. His words go like an arrow to their target, he touches each private wound on the raw, liberating the mass unconscious, expressing its innermost aspirations, telling it what it most wants to hear [quoted in Bullock, 1962, pp. 373–374].*

The seventh chapter of Alan Bullock's masterly biography of Adolf Hitler, from which this quotation is taken, is a study of a dictator's deception of an entire nation. In it, Bullock examines the almost incredible facility with which "in the years 1938 to 1941, at the height of success, [Hitler] had succeeded in persuading a great part of the German nation that in him they had found a ruler of more than human qualities, a man of genius raised up by Providence to lead them into the Promised Land" (p. 410). Bullock finds the key to Hitler's success—and to his ultimate destruction—in "his extraordinary capacity for self-dramatization" (p. 375). "Hitler, in fact, was a consummate actor, with the actor's and orator's facility for absorbing himself in a role and convincing himself of the truth of what he was saying at the time he said it" (p. 377). This is the portrait of a man who managed to dramatize, on a world stage, his fantasies of domination and force, the cult of the hero and racial purity, the subordination of the individual and the supremacy of the state, leaving a trail of unprecedented horror behind him:

> *In the Eyrie he had built . . . above the Berghof . . . he would elaborate his fabulous schemes for a vast empire embracing the Eurasian Heartland of the geopoliticians; his plans for breeding a new elite biologically pre-selected; his design for reducing whole nations to slavery in the foundation of his new empire. Such dreams had fascinated Hitler since he wrote* Mein Kampf. *It was easy in the late 1920s and early 1930s to dismiss them as the product of a disordered and over-heated imagination. . . . But these were still the themes of Hitler's table talk in 1941-2 and by then . . . Hitler had shown that he was capable of translating his fantasies into a terrible reality. The invasion of Russia, the S.S. extermination squads, the*

planned elimination of the Jewish race; the treatment of
the Poles and Russians, the Slav Untermenschen—*these,*
too, were the fruits of Hitler's imagination [pp. 374–
375].

The devastating success of Hitler's imposture owed much to
Hitler's cynical manipulation of his image, combined with his
own growing belief in his self-created myth. As the Second
World War continued, he succumbed more and more to
megalomania. He had presented himself as Germany's savior,
the instrument of Providence, the player of a world-historical
role, exempt from the constraints that bound ordinary men, and
gradually he began to believe in his own infallibility. "When he
began to look to the image he had created to work miracles of
its own accord—instead of exploiting it—his gifts deteriorated
and his intuition deluded him. Ironically, failure sprang from
the same capacity which brought him success, his power of self-
dramatization, his ability to convince himself. . . . No man was
ever more surely destroyed by the image he had created than
Adolf Hitler" (p. 385).

At a more profound level, far from being their longed-for
savior, Hitler was strongly aggressive toward his people. Making
a fool of the audience and using lies and deceit can be seen as
aggressive acts, a form of retaliation—in Hitler's case, against
what? His ineffective and violent parents? The sense of betrayal
he felt at Germany's capitulation at the end of the First World
War and the end of the empire? He felt no scruples in demanding
the sacrifice of millions of lives for the cause of Germany during
the Second World War; equally, he was prepared to sacrifice
Germany itself, in the final year of the war, rather than relinquish

power and admit defeat. Albert Speer, Reich Minister for Armaments and War Production, recalls Hitler's reaction when presented with Speer's conviction that the war was lost: "In an icy tone [he] continued: 'If the war is lost, the people will be lost also. It is not necessary to worry about what the German people will need for elemental survival. On the contrary, it is best for us to destroy even these things. For the nation has proved itself to be the weaker, and the future belongs solely to the stronger eastern nation. In any case only those who are inferior will remain after this struggle, for the good have already been killed' " (1970, p. 557).

Two days later, Hitler confirmed this attitude in his order to implement a scorched-earth policy in the face of the advancing allied forces:

> *"All military, transportation, communications, industrial, and supply facilities, as well as resources within the Reich" were to be destroyed. The message was the death sentence for the German people. . . . The consequences would have been inconceivable: For an indefinite period there would have been no electricity, no gas, no pure water, no coal, no transportation. All railroad facilities, canals, locks, docks, ships, and locomotives destroyed. Even where industry had not been demolished, it could not have produced anything for lack of electricity, gas, and water. No storage facilities, no telephone communications—in short, a country thrown back into the Middle Ages [p. 560].*

At the end of his life, Hitler was prepared to lay waste the country he had spent so much time and energy molding to his image of the most technologically and architecturally brilliant, militarily powerful, and culturally imposing on earth. The cynicism, deceit, and brutal exploitation that lay behind his imposture was finally exposed, fatally late in the day.

Yet the spell that this most devastatingly seductive of Pied Pipers cast over his followers survived, battered but more or less intact, until the end. It compelled Speer, disgraced and demoted, to risk his life and return to Berlin to say a last goodbye to the Fuhrer:

> *The overpowering desire to see him once more betrays the ambivalence of my feelings. For rationally I was convinced that it was urgently necessary, although already much too late, for Hitler's life to come to an end. Underlying everything I had done to oppose him in the past months had been the desire to prevent the annihilation that Hitler seemed bent on. . . . I was now awaiting his death impatiently. . . . And yet that very expectation brought out once again my emotional bond to Hitler. . . . My feelings of pity for the fallen ruler were growing stronger and stronger. . . . On the one hand there was sense of duty, oath of allegiance, loyalty, gratitude—on the other hand the bitterness at personal tragedy and national disaster—both centered around one person: Hitler [pp. 601–602].*

It was many more years before Speer was able to come to terms with the ambivalence of his personal feelings and to grasp the full extent of Hitler's imposture on the German people—years of self-enforced introspection during the twenty years he served in Spandau jail:

August 24, 1960. . . . *Going over it all in Spandau, I have gradually understood completely that the man I served was not a well-meaning tribune of the masses, not the rebuilder of German grandeur, and also not the failed conqueror of a vast European empire, but a pathological hater. The people who loved him, the German greatness he always talked about, the Reich he conjured up as a vision—all that ultimately meant nothing to him. I can still recall the astonishment with which I read the final sentence of his testament. In the midst of an apocalyptic doom it attempted to commit us all to a miserable hatred of the Jews [1976, pp. 353–354].*

Shades of Imposture

Imposture, of course, does not always operate at such extremes of tragedy and corruption. As I stated earlier evidence suggests that imposture may be a personality characteristic that manifests itself in a variety of ways, ranging from feelings of incompetence and phoniness to deliberate fraud. The repercussions these manifestations can have on organizational life, which is our main preoccupation here, have a correspondingly wide range.

Feeling Imposturous

At various times, a distinction has been made between the "true" and the "neurotic" impostor (Greenacre, [1958] 1971a, [1958] 1971b; Aarons, 1959; Gediman, 1985). True impostors are people whose identity is based on impersonation rather than on actual attainments and accomplishments. Neurotic impostors are those individuals who feel fraudulent and imposturous while actually being successful. These people have an abiding feeling that they have fooled everyone and are not as competent and intelligent as others think they are. They attribute their success to luck, compensatory hard work, or superficial factors such as physical attractiveness and likeability. Some are incredibly hardworking, always overprepared. However, they are unable to accept that they have intellectual gifts and ability. They live in constant fear that their imposturous existence will be exposed—that they will not be able to measure up to others' expectations and that catastrophe will follow.

To take an example: a prominent female executive in Holland, a country not generally known for having many women in top positions, described to me her experience of having both a career and family life:

> *When I decided to go to university and study business economics most people looked at it as a passing whim, a few years of study at the most, a good way of finding a husband. I actually did find a husband but continued my studies and received a degree. To do that and have a baby as well was relatively unheard of at the time. I certainly got an earful. . . . But what really became an irritant to many was my decision to work. How could I do that as a mother? How could I live with myself? I think most people considered me quite irresponsible.*
>
> *I was exposed to a lot of pressures and, of course, I had to deal with my own memories of the role my mother had played when I was growing up. She had been a typical housewife. Not staying at home and pursuing a career*

obviously made me a bad mother. Fortunately, it is now more common to have a career and a family life in Holland. But at that time there was a lot of pressure on me to quit.

In spite of my success in business and what I think has been a good family life, I still have my doubts about doing both. The symptom is that—in spite of all my efforts to fight it—I constantly feel guilty. I have always lived with the sense that I am not really good at anything. Men may find it hard to understand what I am talking about.

One of the psychological tasks of childhood is to ensure that "the infant's primary narcissism, the belief in his own and in his parents' omnipotence, . . . gradually recede[s], that is to say, it must be replaced by autonomous functioning" (Mahler, Pine, and Bergman, 1975, p. 226). Individuals who feel imposturous frequently experience difficulties in establishing this process of separation/individuation. They never feel truly independent; they lack a cohesive sense of self. Their achievements and capabilities are experienced as phony and cause guilt, fear, and stress. They consider themselves frauds (Clance and Imes, 1978; Clance, 1985). Such people are unusually sensitive to rejection, afraid of social failure, and suffer from residual dependence needs. They have notably perfectionist attitudes toward themselves. It is as if they have incorporated the excessive expectations of their parents, without their being properly internalized. They frequently suffer from anxiety, lack of self-confidence, and depression.

In the case of women who feel imposturous, Clance and Imes (1978) hypothesize the existence of two types, depending on their family history. According to their study, the first type is victimized by a family in which one sibling is designated the clever one, while the sibling who will later feel impostorous is called the sensitive, or socially adept, one. In spite of her string of achievements, the family continues to attribute greater brilliance and ability to the "clever" sibling, whose academic performance is often in fact much poorer. This attribution leaves the "sensitive" sibling doubting her true abilities and questioning whether her family, despite all the external evidence, might not after all be right. In the second situation, the person who feels impostorous is asserted to be superior in every way—intellect, personality, appearance. Many anecdotes are repeated about her precocity as an infant. Yet, at the same time, she has difficulty achieving. Given the indiscriminate manner in which she is praised, she begins to distrust her parents', and consequently her own, perceptions.

Although one can argue that the attribution of ability is subject to sex stereotyping—women are defined by society as less competent than men, and some women worry that their success will jeopardize their relationships with men and their competence as mothers—one can seriously question whether feeling impostorous is limited to women. Men may suffer from similar feelings, often related to their unconscious guilt at doing better than their father. This guilt may lead to anxiety induced by fear of his envy (Schafer, 1984). In such instances, it seems that the oedipal drama has never been successfully resolved. These infantile fears—which may contain a kernel of truth, often based on covert messages—may linger on into adulthood (Kets de Vries, 1989). These feelings can grow, as success frequently projects people into a style of life very different from their families', raising realistic fears of separation, estrangement, and rejection. However, with respect to the gender question there is one caveat worth mentioning, and it concerns sexuality. Although it is almost impossible for a man to fake orgasm, this form of imposture is quite easy for women. Women who experience difficulties in reaching orgasm, or for various reasons resort to faking it, may feel imposturous in other areas of their life.

Like the true impostor, people who feel imposturous may adopt a survival strategy based on inauthenticity in order to win the approval of others: through sycophancy, intellectual flattery, and charm they can avoid the social rejection they dread. Again as with the true impostor, the strain of maintaining this false front can cause it to break down. Instead of merely feeling fraudulent, these people may engage in self-defeating acts, achieving, as it were, "victory through defeat" (Reik, 1941) and having their conviction of imposture confirmed by their own foolish actions. This behavior may conform to an attention-seeking pattern established in the individual's past. Women, in particular, may demonstrate what has been called "the Cinderella complex" (Dowling, 1981), in which self-defeat indicates a deep-rooted wish to be taken care of or rescued from the responsibility of having to take care of oneself. Waiting for one's prince to come, however, can be a costly strategy.

Overall, the effects of feeling imposturous can have serious implications for both the individual and the organization. The vicious circle of feelings of inadequacy, overcompensatory hard work, procrastination (fear of taking action), doubt, and guilt can be extremely difficult to break. The manifestation of such feelings can lead to functional paralysis or disastrously self-defeating acts and, in an organizational context, the consequences can be far-reaching.

Being Imposturous

I suggested earlier that to some extent we are all impostors—we are all on stage. Our role playing becomes prominent when we act in a public setting such as an organization (Goffman, 1971). Entrepreneurs, in particular, possess many of the qualities found in the impostor: after all, entrepreneurs, like impostors, are trying to turn their fantasies into reality. In their intense need to pursue a vision and convince others of their ideas, they may resort to a distortion of the facts. Nevertheless, the enthusiasm they generate in selling their dreams—unrealistic or ill-defined as they may be—is important because through it they can be catalysts for change and, if successful, agents of economic improvement.

Sometimes, however, the dreams turn sour. One of the most dramatic recent examples of imposture in business enterprise is the case of Refaat El-Sayed, the former chairman of the Swedish biotechnology firm Fermenta. El-Sayed dazzled the Swedish financial and industrial establishment, the media, and the public at large. He became a folk hero because of his unpretentious life-style and his apparent indifference to the trappings of wealth, even after becoming the richest man in Sweden. He was photographed in his small apartment in a Stockholm suburb drinking Coca-Cola and eating pizza; he played soccer with an amateur team. He was the inspiration and pride of Sweden's large immigrant population. He was voted "Swede of the Year" in 1985 by Swedish television. Unfortunately, what initially looked like a storm in a teacup—the revelation that he had never, as he claimed, held a doctorate—turned into a full-blown scandal when an increasing number of irregularities in his life were revealed. Fermenta stock, once the darling of the investment community, plunged by more than 90 percent in one year, damaging many individuals and Swedish institutions (Wittebort, 1987; Sundqvist, 1987). It is worth looking closely at El-Sayed's career in order to appreciate the full extent and consequences of imposture at this level.

Little is known of El-Sayed's early days, and he has not always been helpful in setting the record straight. It seems, however, that he was born in Egypt in 1946, the youngest of five children and the son of a teacher. His mother, who came from Czechoslovakia, died a year after his birth. According to El-Sayed, two of his brothers died in the war with Israel. His father remarried and had nine more children. As a teenager, El-Sayed went twice to Czechoslovakia to participate in a youth camp. In 1966 he left Egypt for Sweden, in order to go to university. While in Sweden he visited the Soviet Union a number of times, again in order to go to summer camp. In 1972 he married a Swedish social worker.

Whatever the mix of fact and fantasy in El-Sayed's account of his early life, one thing is clear: it was confusing and turbulent. The loss of his mother when he was so small must have had a serious impact on the family; her coming from such a different cultural background must have been a source of curiosity to him. The confusion was intensified by the presence of a stepmother and more siblings. We can only conjecture about the role played by the different female figures in El-Sayed's life. Not much is said about his father, but, according to El-Sayed, his paternal grandfather was important in influencing his ideas and values.

If we are to believe El-Sayed's account, he was forced at an early age to be self-sufficient and to conduct himself like a small adult. We can infer from this that age-appropriate development was disrupted. He learned early in his life to be a survivor, to take the initiative, and to be self-reliant. He has described how he recognized early on his ability to capture the attention of others, to bring them under his spell, and to assume a leadership role.

Although we will never know the exact nature of the family dynamics, we can deduce that El-Sayed's visits to Czechoslovakia and Russia and his eventual emigration to Sweden were ways of coming to grips with who he really was, attempts to stabilize a confused sense of personal and cultural identity. His later behavior shows, however, that this sense of confusion may have lingered on and also demonstrates the difficulty he had in distinguishing fact from fiction. The wish to believe, to fabricate new truths to cover painful reality and fit the facts to match his desires, may have become so strong that it marred his sense of reality. The demands of psychological survival imposed at such an early age may have turned into a life theme.

Early in his business career, El-Sayed showed strong entrepreneurial inclinations. He worked as a consultant in microbiology and held several patents. In 1973 he started a company called Micro-Chem, where he formed contacts he found advantageous later on. In 1981 he became interested in a penicillin factory owned by Astra, a Swedish pharmaceutical company. The factory, Fermenta, was losing money, and Astra was willing to sell. Through ingenious misrepresentation of his finances—he did not, in fact, have any money—and a number of imaginative tax maneuvers, El-Sayed gained control of Fermenta, paying one Swedish crown for the shares. At that time, Fermenta was making the raw material needed for the production of penicillin, a depressed market with worldwide overcapacity. El-Sayed's original idea was to turn the factory into a producer of cattle vaccine, a product that yielded high margins. However, he never pursued this idea, preferring instead to continue to buy various antibiotics firms.

Surprisingly enough, Fermenta started to make profits, due to a large extent to beneficial currency fluctuations. In 1984, El-Sayed decided to take Fermenta public. The prospectus stated—possibly to increase his credibility—that he had a Ph.D. in chemistry. Fermenta shares were floated at a time when the Swedish stock market was experiencing an unprecedented rise. Furthermore, there were few biotechnology companies in Sweden. The share issue was sixteen times oversubscribed.

From all descriptions, El-Sayed was a fireball, a man in a hurry, totally future-oriented. Some even portrayed him as a continuously moving target, a characteristic that may have made him hard to pin down and understand. His speech was rapid, fragmented, heavily accented, and often incoherent. His mannerisms and unorthodox behavior puzzled many, but others labeled him a genius simply because of the mystique generated by their inability to understand him. In Sweden, where people characteristically have different modi operandi, this unconventional outsider left his audience completely spellbound. He had an uncanny knack for harnessing others' involvement. El-Sayed was also described as extremely talented in reading other people. His warmth and generosity were attractive, and he had the ability to appear to give each person with whom he came into contact exactly what that person wanted. His command of figures and statistics, a quality that made him a successful negotiator, was dazzling. However, with hindsight it appears that many of his presentations were incorrect and that he often took advantage of the impact he made on people. Paradoxically, El-Sayed's antiheroic pose drew more attention to him than might otherwise have been the case. It was an effective way of satisfying his need to be liked and popular. In the end, as a spokesman for Volvo said, ascribing more deliberate planning to El-Sayed's actions than was probably the case, he "more or less fooled all of Swedish society—politicians, businessmen, financial analysts, financial journalists" (quoted in Wittebort, 1987, p. 96).

The year 1985 was a time of rapid expansion for Fermenta. El-Sayed frantically bought up new companies and entered into joint ventures and marketing arrangements with companies in related areas. His aim was to become a major player in the antibiotics field, so that he could influence world prices. In the meantime, he succeeded in attracting some of the most reputable businessmen in Sweden to his board of directors. By the end of 1985, El-Sayed had become the richest man in Sweden—on paper, at least; he reached the zenith of his career in January 1986 with the announcement of a spectacular deal. With Volvo's backing, Fermenta would take the lead in consolidating Sweden's pharmaceutical and biotechnology industry, thereby gaining control over some of the major competing companies.

Soon after this announcement an innocuous-looking article appeared in an obscure newspaper, questioning whether El-Sayed had obtained a doctorate. For many, this small deception was hard to take. After initial disbelief, those involved started to take a close look at El-Sayed's various activities. The Volvo deal fell through, and the "socialist dream," as El-Sayed had been called because of his ability to play a capitalist game with a socialist touch, tumbled rapidly from his pedestal. An increasing number of irregularities were exposed—long-term contracts paid up front, capital transactions recorded as profits, buy-back arrangements of Fermenta shares made at guaranteed profits, and loans issued to El-Sayed himself for other questionable transactions. It became clear that Fermenta had operated with imprecise reporting and selective forecasting. Industrivarden, an investment company affiliated with Svenska Handelsbanken, discovered that Fermenta's assets were vastly overvalued. It also emerged that a part of Fermenta's profits were generated by deals that never existed. And it became clear, too, that El-Sayed had played an active role in managing Fermenta's stock price. He had been a true master of the media, playing his rags-to-riches story for all it was worth. Any journalist willing to listen had received stories about future deals, mergers, and acquisitions—announcements that could not help but influence the stock price. Eventually, everyone realized that what El-Sayed sold were dreams and promises, that the stock price of Fermenta was to a large extent built on air rather than substance, and that his company, far from being a high-tech firm, was a simple manufacturing enterprise.

El-Sayed displays many of the characteristics of the impostor: his showmanship, his verbal virtuosity, his talent for capitalizing on the greed of others, his ability to get his audience to suspend disbelief, and his capacity to create excitement about the proposed success of his ventures. The protean quality of his own shaky sense of identity is indicated in the way in which he oscillated between playing the roles of business tycoon and just-average guy. The way in which he mixed fact and fantasy indicates that his capacity for reality testing was to some extent marred. His lie about his credentials was certainly self-destructive. Given the high level of self-generated public attention to which he was exposed, it was almost inevitable that he would be found out.

Apparently El-Sayed failed to see anything wrong with his actions. As with many entrepreneurs, setting boundaries, distinguishing between what was his and what was the company's, was not his forte. He probably rationalized that he was acting in the best interests of the company, and at one level of analysis that may have been correct. He does not appear personally to have benefited greatly from all his wheeling and dealing. In fact, El-Sayed's identification with Fermenta was so strong that he was unwilling to sever his connection with it and enrich himself by selling out at a time when a deal was still possible. A personal encounter with El-Sayed reinforces my belief that in many ways his behavior was not very different from that of the typical entrepreneur. All entrepreneurs need dreams, but in dreaming they sometimes have difficulty in distinguishing fact from fantasy. In an attempt to resolve his own inner confusion, El-Sayed seems to have transgressed. His personal myth increasingly led him into trouble. His personal problems and those of his business became intertwined. His self-deception eventually led to his downfall.

El-Sayed is now being blamed for the shattered illusions of his investors. As is often the case, a villain is being made out of a former hero. It could be argued, however, that the investors are not blameless themselves, having become victims of their own greed. When he could no longer deliver, El-Sayed was made into a scapegoat. Although we may hypothesize that he did not act wholly intentionally but was swept away by unconscious forces, he was convicted by a Stockholm court on fourteen counts of financial misconduct and given a five-year prison term ("From Rags to Riches to Penitentiary," 1989, p. 12).

As a postscript to El-Sayed's story, it should be added that people like him are to a large extent the lifeblood of society; they see new possibilities where others fail to do so and help to reevaluate existing practices and patterns. His rather ironic legacy to his adopted country is that the scandal has inspired radical and lasting changes in the Swedish financial system.

Dealing with Imposture

G. K. Chesterton once remarked that "a really accomplished impostor is the most wretched of geniuses; he is Napoleon on a desert island." However, as we have seen, most impostors are not that accomplished—they do not remain Napoleons for long. Eventually their hidden flaws surface and they unmask themselves; their problems with reality testing give them away.

The challenge for all of us is to maintain our capacity for reality testing and not to be swept away by emotional forces when the sirens promising instant love, wealth, and happiness beckon and tempt us to give in. When we are faced with promises or assurances that do not make sense, but nevertheless tempt us to suspend our disbelief, we should listen to the warning sounds and take a long, hard look at them. It is not easy to resist the individual who signals, "Trust me, I'll take care of all your needs," and it is particularly difficult to recognize and fight the force of greed. But when these feelings are appealed to, or awakened, it is time to stand back, examine, consult, and assess.

The mesmerism of the impostor is not the only issue we have to deal with. We also have to come to grips with our own feelings of imposturousness. In its own way, this feeling can also have damaging effects on personal and organizational functioning. At times, we all fall victim to negative thoughts and self-doubt. When these become a grinding preoccupation, however, they can spell a miserable life for the individual and those close to him or her. A great deal of time and effort is needed in order for the individual to recapture a sense of authenticity. This change is difficult but not impossible if we are prepared, and given the opportunity, to acquire insight into our motivations and actions. The development of one's reflective capacity and the awareness of one's blind spots can have a prophylactic effect on both the mesmerizing power of the impostor and the paralyzing effects of feeling imposturous.

chapter 7

LEADERSHIP AND THE ABUSE OF POWER:

beyond complicity

*Over the years, I have developed profound sympathy
especially for politicians attempting to survive in a democracy.
From time to time, I would cast envious glances at a variety of
totalitarian models of government ranging from Albania
to North Korea. How much easier to be an effective leader
in that milieu; no wonder those chaps stay in office forever,
or at least until they get shot.*
—Henry Rosovsky,
The University: An Owner's Manual

*t*he most extreme example of the
abuse of power we have witnessed in recent times is the establishment of the concentration and extermination camps in the Nazi
European territories in the 1930s and 1940s. The realities of the
conditions in those camps, revealed after the end of the Second
World War, provide the moral yardstick by which we judge all
events subsequent to that time—and even, with a historical
perspective, those preceding it. Furthermore, they have forced
every individual to reassess his or her ideas of personal responsibility. The responses range from denial to disbelief to grief for
succeeding generations, even in those whose personal links to

that period are severed as great-grandparents, grandparents, and parents, those in whose lifetimes these events happened, themselves disappear. The questions, however, remain: How did it happen? How was it possible? How could people do this to one another?

The answers lie deep in the human psyche. The appalling success of the German camps was due largely to the understanding and relentless misapplication of principles of psychology. The only way to approach an answer to the enduring question of how such things could have happened is to follow a similar path, to look into the workings of the human mind under the influence of such extreme tyranny and, by understanding the processes at work, to find the means to fight them. The psychologist Bruno Bettelheim, who was imprisoned for a year in Dachau and Buchenwald concentration camps before the outbreak of the war, set out to understand these processes in his book *The Informed Heart*, a study of the psychological consequences of living with extreme fear and terror:

> *My approach . . . has been guided by Freud's insights into the role which our unconscious plays in motivating human actions, and by his discovery of the darkest aspects of our minds. Only if we do not close ourselves to these but accept their existence will we be convinced of how important it is to control these our destructive tendencies; thus we may be able to prevent catastrophes such as that from which my generation suffered. . . .*
>
> *We ought not to forget or distort the meaning of Nazi terrorism and genocide; not because of the terrible things which were done by average people to average persons a*

*generation ago, but because of the warning these events
hold for man of today [1986, p. xiii].*

Both inside and outside the camps, the aim of the Nazi state
was the complete subjugation of the individual. Only the long-
and short-term ends differed: in the long term, the flourishing
of the one-thousand-year Reich, and, in the short term, the
harnessing of slave labor for German prosperity and, later, the
war effort. The techniques employed were similar; they were
based on fear, menace, and a cruel complicity forced on individuals, leading them to deny the evidence of their own senses,
emotions, and intellect. The concentration camps, wrote
Bettelheim, "threw all tendencies of the state into bolder relief"
(p. 240). Within the camps, prisoners were systematically
stripped of personal possessions and personal identity, their
names were no longer recognized, and they were referred to only
as numbers. They were denied even the most elementary sanita-
tion facilities and were frequently obliged to soil themselves,
which made it easy for those overseeing them to classify the
victims as subhuman and to rationalize any atrocity. Every form
of humanity was taken away from these smelly, undernourished
caricatures. This process simplified the process of "splitting":
Ubermensch (the Germanic ideal bodily type) versus *Untermensch*.
The individual was swiftly subsumed into the mass; any overt
signs of a surviving individualism were punished harshly. It was
a rapid process of self-elimination, "a deliberate effort to speed
their decline from self-respecting adults to obedient children"
(p. 134): "Both the prisoner's self-interest and SS pressure
worked in the same direction. To remain independent implied
dangers and many hardships; to comply with the SS seemed in

the prisoner's own interest, because it automatically made life easier for him. Similar mechanisms were at work in the inhabitants of Germany outside the concentration camps, though not quite in such obvious form" (pp. 135–136).

The ultimate result of this process, among the prisoners who survived long enough, "was a personality structure willing and able to accept SS values and behavior as its own" (p. 169):

> *From copying SS verbal aggressions to copying their form of bodily aggression was one more step, but it took several years to reach that. It was not unusual, when prisoners were in charge of others, to find old prisoners . . . behaving worse than the SS. . . .*
>
> *Old prisoners tended to identify with the SS not only in their goals and values, but even in appearance. They tried to arrogate to themselves old pieces of SS uniforms, and when that was not possible they tried to sew and mend their prison garb until it resembled the uniforms. . . .*
>
> *Since old prisoners had accepted, or been forced to accept, a childlike dependency on the SS, many of them seemed to want to feel that at least some of the people they were accepting as all-powerful father images were just and kind. Therefore, strange as it may seem, they also had positive feelings towards the SS [pp. 171–172].*

This process of identifying with the aggressor arises from the overwhelming need of individuals to retain some element of psychological security. In this special form of identification individuals, by impersonating the aggressor, assume the aggressor's attributes and may transform themselves from those who are threatened to those making the threat. The potential victims hope to acquire some of the power that the would-be aggressor possesses (Freud, 1966). Bettelheim explored the way in which this process worked among the majority of the German people and concluded: "The more absolute the tyranny, the more debilitated the subject, the more tempting to him to 'regain' strength by becoming part of the tyranny and thus enjoy its power. In accepting all this one can attain, or re-attain, some inner integration through conformity. But the price one must pay is to identify with the tyranny without reservation; in brief, to give up autonomy" (p. 294).

If the Nazi concentration camps represent the ultimate distillation of the effects of oppression by a mass state, the techniques deployed by many totalitarian systems to control their subjects reveal a similar abuse of psychological method. In the aftermath of the collapse of the Communist states of Eastern Europe in the late 1980s, many countries faced the painful process of uncovering and dismantling the pervasive secret security systems that had repressed and controlled the population for many years. For the former citizens of East Germany, revelations of the true extent of the activity of the Stasi, or secret police, had a devastating effect. With the Stasi files opened, they could see how friends spied on friends, husbands informed on wives, and children were set against their parents: "By watching everyone and drawing as many as possible into the process, [the system] largely achieved its purpose, which was to enforce outward conformity on a whole society. Only a few brave individuals were willing to pay the heavy price of opposition, which included prison, social isolation, miserable employment, no foreign travel and often, most painful of all, denial of educational and career opportunities for their children" ("Days of Reckoning," 1992, p. 20). The information system within their country was so intricately woven into the fabric of society that, as they struggle to reconstruct their state and bring the guilty to justice, one of the major problems faced by the East Germans is where to draw the line between the guilty and the innocent and how to decide where responsibility begins and ends when the extent of complicity ranges from the deliberate silence of some citizens to the repressive orders of party officials.

In *Power of the Powerless* (1990), Vaclav Havel wrote: "In everyone there is some willingness to merge with the anonymous crowd and to flow comfortably along with it down the river of pseudo-life." In this chapter I will look at ways in which people in positions of power exploit this universal human tendency. The years 1990 and 1991 brought to public attention two outstanding incidents of the abuse of power by leaders in wildly divergent and dissimilar contexts. The first was Saddam Hussein, president of Iraq, who early in 1991 led his country into the second of two bloody wars he initiated and subsequently lost in the space of a decade. The second was Robert Maxwell, whose complicated business empire collapsed spectacularly within days of his death in November 1991, rocking the business world and making headlines in national and international newspapers for several weeks afterward. I would like to make an immediate disclaimer that I am not associating or equating Maxwell's activities, or the extent of their consequences, with those of Hussein or (considering how this chapter begins) with those of the Nazi state. Instead, I want to look at the effects of the abuse of power in different circumstances and contexts and to examine how the darker sides of human nature manifest themselves in a variety of situations.

When Political Leaders Abuse Power: The Case of Saddam Hussein

As we saw earlier in relation to the excesses of the Nazi state, tyrants force regressive, childlike behavior and dependence on their people. The dynamics of their world are simple: people are either for them or against them in a world of black and white. There is no room for nuances. Independent thinkers cannot survive; those who do not collaborate immediately become the new villains; deviants from the leaders' ideals are assigned an inferior, subhuman status and are targets for their anger.

Most people quickly fall in line and collude, either passively or actively, with the leader's victimization of those who are not prepared to conform. This behavior is self-protective in two ways. First, it limits the possibility that one will become a victim of the leader oneself. Second, as we have seen, identifying with the aggressor is a way of resolving one's sense of helplessness and powerlessness in the face of totalitarianism. Feeling close to the leader—becoming part of the system—creates the illusion of being powerful oneself. This process of identification with the aggressor, the inducement to participate in a form of groupthink, is accompanied by certain required actions, the least subtle of which is participation in the violence directed toward the aggressor's designated enemies. Sharing the guilt in this way becomes a sign of commitment that the leader can feed by making an endless supply of people into villains. The majority of followers, torn between love and fear of their leader, will submit to the demands made of them. They are presented with many handy scapegoats on whom to enact group revenge when things do not go the way the leader wants—tangible entities on which to project everything of which they are afraid, everything that is perceived as evil and threatening to the system. Such a development can have terrifying results. It can lead to the complete self-destruction of an organization or, in the case of a political leader, to the end of an entire nation. We can see this process at work in the Iraq of Saddam Hussein.

It is difficult to separate truth from fiction in the rather murky accounts we have of Hussein's history, mainly because he has assiduously muddied the truth and invented large portions of his own personal myth. We do know that he was born in 1937 in the desert town of Tikrit and that his family was extremely poor (Darwish and Alexander, 1991; Rayski, 1991; Karsh and Rautsi, 1991). His name means "the one who confronts"—an ominous indication of things to come. He never knew his father, who is variously said to have disappeared, died, or been murdered before Saddam's birth. His mother, left husbandless for whatever reason, was also mourning the recent death of her oldest son: all in all, it was not an auspicious start for the new baby. We can speculate that the formidable burden imposed on a child who begins life with a dead or absent parent, combined with the probable ambivalence of his mother's feelings toward him and, later, his stepfather's violence toward him, reinforced Hussein's awareness of himself as an unwanted child. His was a childhood filled with anger, verbal abuse, violence, and crime. Deprived of an education by his stepfather, who sent him out to steal, Hussein ran away from home at the age of eight to go to school.

So runs the official version. It is said that by the age of ten he was familiar with the use of guns and may even have carried one from this point.

There is not usually much hope that an individual starting from such a disadvantaged beginning will make something of his life—unless there is someone who shows interest in the developing child. In Hussein's case, this role seems to have been played by his mother's brother, Khayrallah Tulfah, a schoolteacher in Baghdad. Tulfah had been thrown out of the Iraqi army because of the role he played in an abortive pro-Nazi coup that was suppressed by the British forces in the Second World War. This event gave him a lifelong hatred of Britain and "imperialism," which was absorbed by his nephew. Hussein's ambition was to become an army officer himself—a military career was the only guarantee of upward mobility in Iraq at that time, as the country was torn apart by coups and countercoups. However, Hussein's poor grades kept him out of Baghdad's military academy, a disappointment for which he compensated by proclaiming himself a field-marshal when he came to power.

Early on, Hussein steeped himself in the political plotting that characterized Iraq's turbulent internal affairs. In 1956 he participated in an attempted coup against the Iraqi monarchy, and a year later, when he was twenty, he joined the Baath party, which was to become the state's political organization. The Baath party professes a kind of socialist pan-Arabic ideology but is actually based on ideas of German national socialism and Italian fascism. From his school years onward, Hussein seems to have had no personal life outside the Baath party.

Hussein first came to prominence when, with his uncle, he attempted to assassinate the then ruler of Iraq, General Abd al-

Karim Qasim. The official account of this incident refers to Hussein's willingness to make sacrifices to the point of martyrdom in order to end an unacceptable regime. We see the beginnings of the merging of man and myth in a tale of fearlessness, shrewdness, loyalty to party and people, and iron discipline. When Qasim was finally eliminated, the Baath party came to power, and Hussein was promoted to the Regional Command Council, where he led a special force responsible for terror and assassination. He became an interrogator and torturer in the Qasr al-Nihayyat, or Palace of the End, so-called because it was the place where King Faisal and his family had been gunned down. Hussein set about building up the party's internal security system, the Jihaz Haneen, or "instrument of yearning." His power increased until he became deputy secretary-general of the Revolutionary Command Council (the real power in the country), behind his cousin, General Ahmad Hasan al-Bakr, who was president. In 1968 and 1969 a series of major purges took place in Iraq, including a number of executions in Baghdad's Liberation Square, where fourteen alleged spies were publicly hanged.

On National Day, July 17, 1979, Hussein declared himself president, taking the place of his cousin, who had resigned the previous day, supposedly because of ill health. Five days later, Hussein initiated a dramatic purge among party members in order to rid himself of potential rivals. At a meeting of over one thousand members of the Baath party, he indicated names on a list and obliged each person selected to read out a confession of alleged participation in Syrian-backed plots against Iraq and the party. The terror-stricken remainder responded by shouting "Long live Saddam" and "Death to the traitors" (Darwish and

Alexander, 1991; Karsh and Rautsi, 1991)—the processes of identification with the aggressor and shared guilt were already at work. To reinforce his message, Hussein had this event filmed and had copies distributed to top officials in the Baath party and military. Afterward, twenty-two of the selected "conspirators" were sentenced to death by "democratic execution"—that is, firing squads manned by their fellow party members, including Hussein. Others received lengthy prison sentences. The fabrication of plots and the use of terror would become major weapons in Hussein's campaign to align the masses behind his leadership.

From all the information available, we can infer that Hussein's inner world is one of grandiosity and violence. His paranoia, exacerbated by a volatile political tradition typified by coups and countercoups, is evident and is seen most clearly in his creation of a particularly bloody form of totalitarianism; Iraq is run exclusively by the Baath party, which is in turn controlled entirely by him. The population is kept in check by the activities of the secret police, who enforce policy through torture and who punish in various ways a constant stream of "enemies of the people" to demonstrate the dangers of failing to conform to the regime. Informers are everywhere, ready to report any suspicious activity. The regime Hussein has created strongly resembles that of Stalin, who is, incidentally, one of his heroes. We can speculate that Hussein's actions reflect the violence within him. We see it in his preoccupation with the elimination of potential opponents, in his hit squads, which are sent all over the world, in the gassing of his own citizens, in his treatment of the Kurds and Shi'ite Muslims in Iraq. Above all, it can be seen in the innumerable dead of the two wars he has begun and lost since he took power.

But what does Hussein want? What motivates him? He would say that he is searching for a new kind of world order, a renaissance of the Arab nation. When interviewed at the height of his power, he dwelled nostalgically on the fact that his whole region was once the shining light for other civilizations, that the Arab nation was "the source of all prophets and the cradle of civilization" (Matar, 1981, p. 237). He sees it as his mission to unite the Arab peoples against the foreign usurpers and super-powers, a rallying cry that touches a responsive chord in the impoverished and displaced Arab masses. One enemy in particu-lar is singled out—the Zionists. Hussein perceives himself as the successor of previous glorious leaders: Nebuchadnezzar, who brought the bound Jewish slaves back from Palestine, and Saladin.

However, if this is his professed mission, it does not explain or justify the violence, paranoia, and rampant narcissism with which his life is filled. Concepts like *narcissism* and *grandiosity* are inadequate for explaining the personality cult and enforced adulation that existed in Iraq before operation Desert Storm demonstrated that the idol really had feet of clay. Endless billboards with Hussein's portrait presented him variously as military hero, pre-Biblical warrior, modern nationalist, people's protector, and architect of the modern state. During regular political broadcasts, his name was mentioned thirty to fifty times an hour, with congratulations for his latest achievements. Baghdad's airport is called Saddam International Airport. Iraqi schoolchildren recited his sayings, wore T-shirts printed with his image and wristwatches with his portrait on the face. His picture hung in every house. He was the personification of the ideal Iraqi character, accompanied everywhere by men who, as nearly as possible, were exactly like him in manner, dress, and appearance. Filmed during the Gulf War, he was sometimes hard to distinguish from the moustachioed men in uniform who surrounded him, an admiring gallery of clones. The excesses of his regime forced people into identifying with their aggressor to an almost surreal degree.

Hussein has projected his turbulent inner theater onto his environment, creating a world characterized by violence and megalomania where nobody can be trusted. This projection may be his way of settling his account with his past, of managing his archaic feelings of helplessness, humiliation, and rejection. His paranoia is correspondingly excessive. For fear of their plotting against him, he has eliminated many of his closest collaborators. He is constantly on his guard against assassination attempts. He lives in a world of bunkers, bodyguards, food tasters, and doubles (Brooks and Horwitz, 1991, p. 1). The rare journalist who visits him is stripped naked for a body search, has his hands put in a blue chemical solution to expose or wash away any toxins that may be transferred in a handshake, and surrenders his pen, which is taken apart and checked for hidden weapons.

It was hard to predict where all this abuse of power was tending, what the end would be for Hussein. In the spring of 1991, it seemed that the only alternatives for him were death or disgrace. He had lost "the mother of all battles," the country that he still controlled was deeply divided, and the economy was in ruins. His grief-stricken and demoralized people were openly cursing him as *muka'ab shaytan,* triple devil, and rebellion was raging in fourteen of the eighteen Iraqi provinces. Within weeks, however, he had begun to reassert his authority despite the effects of U.N. sanctions, which hit the Iraqi people hard. A year after the war, infant mortality had trebled, and food and medicine—which would have been supplied if Hussein had agreed to the terms outlined by the U.N. for oil exportation—were scarce. The cowed and terrified Iraqis were again being forced into silence by the reappearance of the secret police. The huge portraits of their president were repaired and were again lining the streets. Opposition was disorganized and fragmented; those who participated in a failed uprising after the Gulf War were tortured and executed with extreme cruelty. Contrary to all Western expectations, Hussein was tightening his hold on Iraq.

Two years after the end of the war, Hussein remained more or less in hiding, reluctant to answer a telephone for fear it would alert Western eavesdroppers to his whereabouts. He changed his cabinet every three weeks. At his rare public appearances, he was protected by no fewer than twenty bodyguards. He was rumored to have at least eighty doubles who acted as decoys when he moved about the country. Nevertheless, his control remained absolute. Hussein's brinkmanship in his attempts to avoid the destruction of his country's chemical and nuclear arsenals were masterly; he teetered constantly on the edge of exhausting the patience of the outside world but rarely overplayed his hand. Postwar reconstruction was also more rapid than Western observers anticipated. Bridges, roads, oil refineries, and public buildings damaged or destroyed in the fighting were almost all rebuilt; public services were restored to prewar performance levels. To the series of enormous billboards celebrating the achievements of the president another was added: "President Saddam Hussein—the symbol of struggle and reconstruction."

The Iraqi army, mistakenly supposed to have been decimated during the fighting, was restored to 40 percent of its prewar capacity, and the south of the country (where postwar rebellion was concentrated) was under martial law. Refugees from Hussein's regime have claimed bitterly for some time that there is an unholy alliance between the Iraqi dictator and the West; that despite all the allied rhetoric during the Gulf War, and despite the encouragement given to Iraqi opposition groups, those behind Operation Desert Storm never intended to destroy Hussein himself; that it is in the long-term political interests of the West to keep Hussein in power, for fear of precipitating a situation that will be worse. For the first time—such is the impact of Hussein's success in reconstructing his country—the same sentiments were being heard on the streets of Baghdad.

It is strikingly obvious that Hussein's resilience should not be underestimated. Unlike other dictators, he is not driven by a political ideology. His main concern is to hold on to power whatever the price may be, and his ability to do so, in the wake of the disasters he has brought to his country, is astonishing. Could anyone have predicted that the boy from Tikrit would turn out the way he did? Could anyone have foreseen that the fit between historical moment (a certain vulnerable time in a nation's development) and one man's personality would lead to such disastrous results? If anybody did say so along the way, they did not survive to repeat their warning. Hussein's infamy, the suffering he has forced on his people, the genocide against the Kurds, the economic ruin of his country, and the disastrous ecological damage he has inflicted on an entire region form a legacy that will stand for a long time.

When Business Leaders Abuse Power: The Case of Robert Maxwell

Although the abuse of power on a national scale can have far-reaching consequences, to which the dead and wounded of the countries participating in the Gulf War bear witness, a certain amount of damage limitation is built into a business setting. When we look at the dramatic collapse of Robert Maxwell's communications business following his death, we are possibly most astonished that the whole extraordinary and complicated edifice could ever have been built in the first place. Certainly, when it fell apart, there was no shortage of financial architects scurrying around pointing out that the foundations had never been sound, that the whole thing was an example of jerry-building on a massive scale. More surprising, it appears that they had been there, saying the same thing, all the time—at least since July 1971, when British Department of Trade investigators decreed that Maxwell "is not in our opinion a person who can be relied upon to exercise proper stewardship of a publicly quoted company" (Bower, 1991, p. 287). Twenty years later, it became clear that Maxwell's fortune was largely ephemeral; that the spectacular results of his companies derived from the juggling of private and public assets or currency trading rather than from solid business transactions; that he had mortgaged nearly every family asset to underwrite his business acquisitions; that to appease his bankers he had been frantically shifting assets and debts from one company to another; that he used company pension funds to help prop up his faltering empire; and that he used shares that he knew to be worthless as collateral for loans. In the furor that followed these revelations, the same questions were asked again and again. Why did nobody stop him? Did nobody understand what he was doing? How did he manage to fool so many people for so long? Why did nobody hear or heed the warnings? The answers to all these questions seem to lie in Maxwell's personality and in the influence he had on his surroundings and the people who worked for him.

In the mass of more or less abusive prose that filled the international press as it charted Maxwell's posthumous exposure, one image occurred repeatedly—that of a cunning, well-fed spider lurking at the center of a large, well-disguised web. This analogy was used to describe Maxwell as both a business and a family man, and his associates and children were alike considered either victims or escapees. The spider image is certainly evocative of the single outstanding characteristic of Maxwell's personality, which could be described as an overwhelming need for control. This need has been universally attributed to the conditions of his life during his first sixteen years.

Maxwell was born Jan Ludvik Hoch in 1923 in a small farming village on the Czechoslovakian-Rumanian border. This area has been described as "the most primitive and impoverished on the whole European continent" (Bower, 1991, p. 12). His parents were Orthodox Jews who had seven children. The family was exceedingly poor but very close, despite the pressures brought to bear by the deprivation of the region in which they lived. In 1939, as the village began to feel the first effects of Nazi anti-Semitism, Maxwell's parents sent him to Budapest to look for work. He never saw any of his family again. They all perished in concentration or extermination camps. Maxwell himself escaped from Hungary and made his way to France, where he fought bravely with Czech forces before being evacuated to

England. He returned to the Continent with the British Army. He distinguished himself through several acts of bravery in intelligence work, frequently behind enemy lines, was commissioned and decorated, and definitively changed his name, after using a number of aliases. In Berlin after the war he first became involved in communications when he was made press chief of the British sector.

By this time Maxwell's mentors in the army and civil service had recognized his extraordinary abilities. He was courageous, intuitive, imaginative, and could speak nine languages fluently. His commanding officer had given him a flattering and revealing recommendation on his transfer into a different regiment: "This man has a very strong personality. He is well-disciplined but will for various reasons give far better results if he has a certain amount of freedom of choice and movement than in a post where he is surrounded by too many rules and restrictions" (quoted in Bower, 1991, p. 26). Tall, charming, extremely handsome, ambitious, and full of dreams for the future, Maxwell in 1945 married Elizabeth Meynard, the daughter of a wealthy French silk manufacturer. They had nine children, of whom seven survived, and from 1946, when Maxwell left the army, they made their home in England.

At the time of their marriage, Maxwell predicted to his wife that he would become a millionaire and a member of parliament, and after returning to England and being naturalized as a British citizen, he set about doing exactly that. After a few false starts, he founded Pergamon Press, with a mandate to publish scientific literature and journals. This solid, rather unexciting publishing company was the base from which Maxwell's eclectic mix of communications acquisitions took off, resulting in the sprawling, highly visible, global media empire he had amassed by the time of his death. Along the way, he achieved his other ambition, and became a Labour MP, living happily with the contradictions of his life as a capitalist socialist, maintaining an inflexibly antagonistic attitude toward the trades unions that supported the political party he represented and with which he was continually at loggerheads in his companies.

Both as an MP and as a businessman, Maxwell was unembarrassed by setbacks and failure. His ability to land on his feet earned him his indelible nickname, "the bouncing Czech." This ability was demonstrated most impressively by his reaction to the 1971 Department of Trade investigation into his handling of the sale of a part of Pergamon's operations. Denouncing the report as "a smear and witch-hunt" (Bower, 1991, p. 287), Maxwell turned to litigation to have the Department of Trade's verdict reversed. It was consistently upheld. However, "ever since, he has insisted that his fight through the courts to reverse their indictment was successful. That is not true, but understanding his persistent and erroneous insistence helps to explain both the inner dilemmas of Maxwell and the environment in Britain in which he desperately sought to succeed" (Bower, 1991, p. 287). The indictment was damning:

> *[Maxwell] is a man of great energy, drive and imagination, but unfortunately an apparent fixation as to his own abilities causes him to ignore the views of others if these are not compatible. . . . Neither his fellow directors, his professional advisers, nor his employees were able to sway his views and actions. The concept of a Board being responsible for policy was alien to him. . . .*

He had a reckless and unjustified optimism which enabled him on some occasions to disregard unpalatable facts and on others to state what he must have known to be untrue [quoted in Bower, 1991, p. 286].

These accusations were unambiguous. Although acknowledging Maxwell's extraordinary talents, the inspectors relentlessly analyzed the ways in which they had been misapplied. The indictment portrays an organizational tyrant, out of touch with reality, satisfying his own narcissistic desires at the cost of truth and caution. Nevertheless, the investigation failed to stop Maxwell. Thereafter, his aim was to control 51 percent of all the companies he was interested in and to ensure that no board of directors, as a result, could call him to account. On to those boards he attracted many top figures in the worlds of finance and politics, people whose concern it should have been to safeguard the interests of the companies and their investors.

Twenty years later, the "unjustified optimism," the lying, the secrecy, the megalomania were finally revealed. How had they been covered up for so long? Is it too easy to attribute it to the "environment in Britain" in the 1970s and boom years of the 1980s? To Maxwell's bulldozing charm and ability to talk himself out of trouble and into favor? By 1991, Maxwell owned companies in Britain, the United States, France, Israel, and Eastern Europe. None was untouched by the catastrophe of his death; many were ruined by it; to all of them it came as a surprise. How was this large-scale deception possible?

As an entrepreneur, Maxwell demonstrated all that ambivalence toward authority that his commanding officer had recognized in 1945. Resentful of rules and restrictions himself, he was tyrannical in imposing them on others. He had to control everyone and everything around him—his family, his employees, his environment. His need for control was reflected in his obsession with security arrangements. Telephones were bugged, coded security locks were fitted to doors, public-address systems were installed through which Maxwell could personally harangue his workforce. When he took over British Printing Corporation, he instituted a system of "unprecedented scrutiny, especially of every penny's expenditure. Only Maxwell could sanction the purchase of a new car or the hire of a temporary secretary, or sign a cheque for over £500" (Bower, 1991, p. 346). Power to him was literally food and drink. At meals in the boardroom, Maxwell was invariably served first, and with the biggest portions, whether sharing a beer-and-sandwiches lunch with trades union representatives or entertaining executives with lobster and champagne.

The ultimate irony of the man who made his fortune through communications was his own compulsive secrecy. As Peter Jay, formerly a top executive in the Maxwell empire, once remarked, "Things were run on a need-to-know principle; if you needed to know, you were not told" (quoted in Cohen, 1991, p. 11). Don Wood, formerly personnel director on the *Daily Mirror,* a Maxwell paper, concurs. Maxwell combined secrecy with his talent alternately to charm or terrorize. This combination, perhaps more than anything else, explains how he managed to continue his fraudulent activities for so long with the more or less enforced collusion of many otherwise respectable people. Maxwell's bad temper was legendary; rumors and apocryphal stories about his quixotic behavior circulated throughout the publishing world. There was enough truth in many of them to increase the atmosphere of fear and dread within the companies he controlled. He had, after all, once sacked his own son Ian for failing to meet him at an airport. Wood describes Maxwell's management style at the *Daily Mirror:*

> *I reported for an early morning meeting at 7.30 or 8.00 a.m. Kevin [Maxwell's youngest son] was often there and would be given a daily lashing. He had not worked long enough for anyone else to know that there were other ways of doing things. . . .*
>
> *Maxwell assumed omnipotent power. We were soldiers. We were given orders and we had to carry them out.*
>
> *Maxwell used charm or fear to get what he wanted. The daily briefings were trenchant. I have seen Kevin reduced to tears on one occasion and, on another, so afraid that he pleaded with me to get some item of information from his father [quoted in Gillie, 1991, p. 17].*

Although Maxwell did not scruple to brutalize his own son in front of other people, presumably as a heavy-handed example of his determination to get his own way, his technique with some of his senior executives was more subtle: "One U.S. banker said he was told by a former top official and director of a Maxwell public company that he and other officer-directors frequently were given only the signing pages of documents for their approval—they were kept in the dark as to the contents of the transactions. The official said that because Maxwell paid them so well, they were often torn between leaving the company or doing the late Mr. Maxwell's bidding" [Wells, Bray, and Reilly, 1991, p. 3].

Many people did leave, of course. But what of those who remained? Cowed by Maxwell's aggression, repressed by his secrecy, beguiled by his incentives and rewards, one could survive in Maxwell's organization only by giving in and keeping quiet. The feelings of helplessness engendered by his abrasive behavior contributed to the escalating tyranny of his management style. Maxwell's corporate culture encouraged collusion with the aggressor through enforced ignorance and acquiescence. The process was paralleled within his own family. The four eldest of his seven surviving children, having made their working debuts in Maxwell's businesses, broke free and have very different life-styles from that of their father. There is no question of the affection or loyalty he inspired in his children. However, home was a forcing house. Ambitious for their success, Maxwell seemed determined to eliminate any resemblance to his own character in his children. They were trained according to his own philosophy of "the three Cs—consideration, concentration and conciseness" (Bower, 1991, p. 115): "Showing politeness, speaking in respectful tones and diligently obeying rules were precisely what Maxwell senior had steadfastly and proudly rejected. Yet he expected those qualities from both employees and his family. Psychologists describe that peculiar characteristic of demanding from others the opposite of your own character as 'projected identification.' Maxwell, one can assume, unconsciously disliked some aspects of his personality and reacted violently if he perceived [them] in others. In his children, he wanted to forestall the development of his own characteristics" (Bower, 1991, p. 115).

Whatever conscious or unconscious motives lay behind Maxwell's way of raising his family, his three youngest children,

Kevin and Ian, and Ghislaine, the daughter after whom Maxwell named the yacht from which he fell to his death, were all working closely with him at the end of his life. Their relationship with their father was not easy. Both Ian and Kevin had left their father's businesses after disagreements but were enticed back. Although not afraid to argue with Maxwell, they found themselves having to cope with the tyrannical demands of a man who could play on the double bond of parent and employer that tied his sons to him: "Good-looking and outgoing, Ian took on his father's abilities as a showman, specializing in marketing and sales. He even took to wearing the unfashionable but colorful bow ties favored by his father. He once said that his father was an impossible act to follow but a marvellous example to emulate in so many ways. At first the act was difficult for him, but he got better at it. . . . Ian . . . flinched but managed to smile his way through the fifteen-hour day" (Gillie, 1991).

Kevin's reaction was different. With him, the process of identification with his aggressor went beyond the choice of necktie. He became far more closely involved than Ian in his father's operations. With his father's aptitude for figures and a similar ruthlessness and entrepreneurial flair, he shared Maxwell's intoxication with the dangers of empire building. In a sixty-fifth birthday tribute to his father, he said: "Above all, you have given me the sense of excitement of having dozens of balls in the air and the thrill of seeing some of them land right" (quoted in Gillie, 1991). Helplessly enmeshed in their father's intrigues, Ian and Kevin Maxwell found their grief at their father's death compounded by the full weight of responsibility for his actions, which landed on their shoulders. The protection of his presence was removed, and they had to face parliamentary inquiries, and possibly the courts, alone. Maxwell once remarked, "My children will not inherit one penny of the wealth I have created" (quoted in Thompson and Delano, 1988). It appears to be one of his few honest predictions.

What does Maxwell's story leave us with, apart from the spectacle of an empire in ruins and the equally sad picture of a shattered family? Many voices, after his death, said, "Told you so"; many more barely concealed their satisfaction that such a monumental figure should have come to such an ignominious end. Yet Maxwell's employees and investors were let down by more than their leader. The regulators of the pension funds that Maxwell rifled were not vigilant enough; bankers, stockbrokers, and investment analysts in the City failed to react; the board members of Maxwell's various companies, for whatever reasons—fear, stupidity, ignorance, or greed—never functioned properly; the numerous accountancy firms involved did not detect his duplicity. Maxwell's litigious reputation admittedly did not help the situation. Many commentators were silenced by his exploitation of Britain's severe libel laws. The media has learned to be wary of him—and it should not be forgotten that he was a major employer in the industry.

In the end, despite the failure of so many different parties to admit that their emperor was marching around naked, the burden of responsibility must rest with Maxwell himself. He was not capable of keeping himself in check, of creating the sort of environment in which others' voices could be heard and listened to. If he had, he might have been a happier man, less driven, less obsessed with the need to control, not constantly teetering between spectacular success and equally spectacular failure, less inclined to live at the extremes, to see his world in terms of black or white, to regard people as either for him or against him. However, these are hypotheses. It was not in his character to act differently; his background could not have taught him differently. General Dwight Eisenhower once said, "You do not lead by hitting people over the head—that's assault, not leadership." But Maxwell was a dispossessed survivor, and a frontal assault on life may have been the only approach that came naturally to him.

The Benevolent Tyrant

Much of Maxwell's behavior demonstrated the darker side of entrepreneurship; the characteristics that were originally a source of strength, and the root of his success, became excessive and led to his eventual downfall. Motivation had been replaced by aggression; inspiration had turned into repression; admiration dissolved into fear, confidence into nervousness; innovation sank into tame acquiescence. The result was an organization that could put up no resistance to the sickness that spread through Maxwell's empire.

When that entrepreneurial energy is well applied, however, nothing can compare with the level of creative activity it engenders. In some circumstances the process of identification with the aggressor—if that aggressor has his or her feet firmly on the ground—is inspirational and enabling, even when the external signs of the process bear a comically alarming resemblance to less healthy manifestations:

> *Something strange has been happening in the Amstrad boardroom. Several directors have sprouted beards. Not the full, ethnic type, more the designer-stubble type and it*

makes them look just like Alan Sugar, the company's chairman. In some instances the resemblance is so strong, they could almost be clones.

"I knew you were going to say that," Ann Sugar, Alan's wife of 24 years, says. "There are a lot of beards there, and I'm sure most of them didn't have them when they joined." Mrs Sugar has an air of resignation when she speaks. She is clearly used to people hero-worshipping her husband, be they colleagues or friends [Leonard, 1992].

Like both Hussein and Maxwell, Alan Sugar has a rags-to-riches background. He grew up on an east London council estate, the youngest of four children, and from the age of twelve earned money by getting up early in the morning to boil beetroots for a local greengrocer. By the time he was sixteen, he was earning more by working in the evenings after school and at weekends than his father earned in a week. He founded Amstrad when he was twenty-one and made his fortune by selling basic, low-cost computers and software to the public, who were just waking up to the novelty of domestic information technology in the early 1980s. At forty, he was the fifteenth richest man in Britain. When his personal fortune was cut by more than two-thirds following the stock-market crash of 1987, he remained philosophical ("It's basically shares, and I have always totally ignored it. It's flattering but you haven't got it and so it's irrelevant") and continued to work with undiminished energy.

In February 1992, a rare interview with Sugar appeared in the London *Times*. Carol Leonard produced from it a profile that might bring to mind many of the characteristics of the late Robert Maxwell; it is debatable, of course, to what extent these are typical traits of the successful entrepreneur. In her profile, Leonard discusses Sugar's legendary short temper ("Ask anybody here about my patience and they will laugh"); his tendency to see things in black and white ("He never allows any room for misunderstanding. Some people call this tunnel vision, say that he is incapable of looking left or right, that he lacks a third dimension"); his need for control and his egotism ("My wife keeps asking me what I'm killing myself for, she says no one will thank me. . . . I suppose it's ego. I might only own 33 per cent, but this company is mine, those are my initials up there, and it's going to be around for ever"). But equally she stresses his honesty, openness, and accessibility: "If you ring the switchboard and ask for him, he will usually pick up the phone himself."

In the late 1980s Amstrad faced numerous difficulties, and its chairman was confronted with accusations of deviousness over acquisitions and maneuverings that seemed to hover between shrewdness and sharp practice. Perhaps the nearest thing approaching scandal to touch Sugar himself was his purchase of Tottenham Hotspur football team, of which he is chairman. In that position, Sugar had a critical vote in awarding the satellite station BSkyB a contract to televise live matches of the newly formed football league. Amstrad sells satellite dishes on behalf of BSkyB, and when it looked as though BSkyB was about to be outbid by ITV, a rival station, Sugar alerted BSkyB to increase its bid. It is a demonstration of Sugar's openness or foolishness that he made the call to BSkyB within the hearing of an ITV representative. Sugar weathered the storm of protest and accusations that followed: "Mr Sugar sees nothing wrong in his double dealing. It plainly wasn't a sealed bid auction, since over the months both sides had been given countless opportunities to outbid the other. In Mr Sugar's eyes it was a no-holds-barred fight to the end, and he believes he cannot be accused of impropriety" ("Alan Sugar's Professional Foul," 1992).

If this attitude shows a certain ruthlessness, it is at least tempered by Sugar's own uncompromising directness. He demonstrated that directness again in his letter to shareholders concerning his long-awaited bid to reprivatize Amstrad after disastrous results in 1992:

> *We created an organization run by management inexperienced in international trade, inventory control, acquisition procedures and manufacturing. For this I must take the lion's share of the blame. . . .*
>
> *In 1989, Amstrad faced the stark reality that its products no longer had the competitive edge which it needed. Amstrad had become a company of the sort we ridiculed in the late 1970s, a high overhead, increasingly sluggish company which offered the same products as its competitors [Bennett, 1992, p. 27].*

His offer to repurchase the company was heavily criticized by shareholders and commentators alike as self-serving and inconsiderate of shareholders, but Sugar held firmly and unrepentantly to his view: "Don't you think some common sense should prevail? Do you honestly think that someone with a high profile like me is going to be allowed to do anything in an incorrect or improper manner? Since the Big Bang and the scandals of the Guinness, Blue Arrow and Polly Peck affairs, as well as the numerous insider dealing cases, lawyers, bankers, and advisers are so cautious that it is a wonder anybody like me is allowed to make a cup of tea, let alone a privatisation offer" (letter to the London *Times,* November 16, 1992).

If there are parallels to be drawn between the successes and failures of both Maxwell and Sugar, such parallels only underline their different responses to similar problems. It is the difference between honesty and dishonesty, shrewd practice and crooked dealing, willingness to accept responsibility for one's actions and refusal to face the reckoning head on. However unpopular or outrageous Sugar's bid to save his company, his hardline approach was perhaps more acceptable than a mysterious disappearance from the stern of a moving yacht in the small hours of the morning.

More than anything else, the *Times* portrait of February 1992 is of a man who has managed to hold on to reality and retain a sense of himself throughout his years of rapid and extraordinary success. He describes himself as "very down to earth."

> *He has, he says, seen people who have let money go to their heads, "and they become different people, they try to force their way into upper circles and I'm just not like that.". . .*
>
> *Sugar is always brutally honest. He will give a straight answer to a straight question. . . . He is aware of his faults but he will not try to correct them. He shrugs his shoulders in lame disagreement when they are detailed. . . . That he is irreverent, rude, and excessively aggressive. That he has an explosive temper and swears, that he hates wimps and needs strong people. At the same time, those who work most directly with him clearly adore him, get a buzz from working alongside him, say that he is scrupulously fair,*

> *does not hold grudges, and describe his management style*
> *as that of a benevolent tyrant"* [Leonard, 1992].

After so many devils, it is good to end this chapter with the portrait of someone more on the side of the angels. The future will tell whether the angel remains angelic. But he has gotten off to a good start. Whatever happens, the rarity of people like Sugar both adds to their value and underlines the duality of the nature of power, the fine balance that has to be found between its constructive use and its abuse, the thin line that separates the inspirational leader from the repressive tyrant.

managing the ambiguities of leadership and power

*The strongest man in the world
is the man who can stand alone.*
—Henrik Ibsen,
An Enemy of the People

*t*his book is a response to clear indications that the issues of leadership and motivation are more important than ever. They are becoming increasingly essential to organizational survival, and in the future it will be up to leaders to recognize the importance of these issues in order to exploit the strengths of their organizations in the right way. It could be said that leaders are in the business of energy management. Their primary task is to find the most effective way of directing the prevailing energy in their organizations toward a common goal. Leaders have to do more than create, out of their inner theater, a vision of the future that is in tune with the external environment. They must also articulate, share, and enact that vision by channeling the existing aggressive energy of their people outward; they must create an environment where this energy is not dissipated in internecine territorial battles and internal political games. The people in their organizations should be encouraged to fight the common enemy, the competition. Leaders should provide a focus for the task at hand. At the same time, emotional energy has to be inwardly generated. People have to be motivated and empowered. They should be encouraged to share their opinions, to engage in contrarian thinking. Last, but not least, they should enjoy themselves at work; people should be able to have fun.

Naturally, such an organizational culture will depend very much on the kind of psychological contract that exists between leader and followers. Without effective energy management a proper psychological contract will be lacking, and with the absence of such a contract will come an absence of trust. Trust is essential for the well-being and proper functioning of organizations. Because the specter of paranoia can raise its ugly head at any time within a large organization, an essential task for any leader is to find a way of managing and negating these destructive forces. Trust depends on communication, support, respect, fairness, credibility, competence, and consistency on the part of the leader. In order for the leader to understand the meaning of these words, it is important that he or she realize what it means to be a follower, how it feels to be in that position. The leader should be equipped with empathy and a capacity for imaginative self-analysis. The degree to which these requirements are met, however, will depend on the leader's personal psychological equilibrium.

Leadership: A Balancing Act

It is cause for concern when a leader's reactions are off-balance or when a leader begins to behave in irrational ways. Quite a few danger signs can be identified, although the following is by no means an exhaustive list: Is there a lack of realism in the leader's vision? Does the leader always find fault with others? Does the leader fail to accept personal responsibility for his mistakes? Does the leader think that people are either for or against her? Do people in the organization find themselves forced into self-censorship because of the leader's adverse reactions to bad news? Do only yeasayers progress in the organization? Does the leader want to make all the decisions herself? Is she blowing her horn all the time? Does she need to be constantly in the limelight? Is she obsessed by her public image? Have suspicion and distrust crept into the organization? Has the leader removed himself too far from day-to-day activities? Is he becoming less accessible? Does he pay too much attention to outside symbols of success and other perks? Is he refusing to plan for leadership succession? If several of these questions can be answered in the affirmative, there will definitely be reason to worry about the organization. The leader's mental health may be off-balance.

What constitutes a balanced person? Many years ago this question was put to Freud, who coined the famous dictum that a "normal" person is the individual who has the capacity for *lieben und arbeiten*—love and work ([1930] 1961). Freud was talking about the individual's capacity for human connectedness, the ability to relate to others, in both an emotional and social context. Other people in the helping professions have tried to elaborate on Freud's definition. For example, the psychoanalyst Reuben Fine (1977) suggests that "man can find happiness if he loves rather than hates, has pleasure, sexual gratification, has a feeling life, yet one guided by reason, an adequate role in the family, a sense of identity, works, is creative, has a role in the social order, is able to communicate and is reasonably free from psychiatric symptoms" (p. 18).

Although some may argue that Fine has a rather utopian view of what people should be like, many of his observations ring true. That many people do not reach his ideal may be due to a number of factors. For example, every individual erects a good number of defenses to maintain a stable, favorable conception of the self. These defenses are used to control impulses or emotions that are deemed unacceptable and that give rise to conflicts: the more vulnerable the psychological equilibrium of the individual, the more formidable the defensive barriers to adaptation and change. In such instances much time and effort are spent on adapting and modifying resultant attitudes, emotions, abilities, and expectations.

An individual's mental health and capacity to cope and adapt are determined by the kind of defenses used. We know that the more a person resorts to rather primitive defensive processes such as splitting (viewing the world and the people inhabiting it as either all good or all bad), idealization (overestimating others), projection (ascribing to others what one rejects in oneself), and denial, the more problematic his or her adaptive capacity (Kernberg, 1975; Paolino, 1981). The adoption of such defenses indicates a tendency to oversimplify attitudinal positions and a need to externalize individual responsibility.

Another criterion of mental balance is stability of identity, the extent to which the person possesses a steady sense of self (Erikson, 1959). The lack of an integrated identity gives rise to marked feelings of unreality, estrangement, puzzlement, anxiety, and emptiness. The contradictory self-images or aspirations that result make it difficult for those affected to perceive themselves as "whole" human beings vis-à-vis others. An unclear differentiation between images of self and others causes a continual blurring of boundaries. In contrast, a strong sense of identity allows individuals to feel good in their skin—that is, in a state of effective balance between their emotional and physiological inner and outer worlds.

Another factor influencing mental health, adaptation, and coping ability is the individual's capacity for reality testing. The ability to distinguish inner from outer reality, fact from fantasy, determines the extent to which behavior, judgment, and feelings can become impaired in stressful situations. The capability for reality testing demonstrates how well a person's cognitive processes are integrated or the extent to which that person's thinking processes are limited to pure wish fulfillment.

Apart from these broad categories, a number of less specific weaknesses may also impede individual adaptation. One of these weaknesses is lack of anxiety tolerance, a deficiency in the way a person responds to stressful situations. Closely related to anxiety tolerance is impulse control. Does an increase in anxiety, or the arousal of a specific need, lead to impulsive action—often unpredictable or erratic—or has the individual sufficient resources at his command in these situations to retain control of himself and his environment? What is the individual's capacity to tolerate depression following loss, frustration, sorrow, rejection, and disappointment? Can she handle these experiences without resorting to destructive and regressive behavior? We could also consider here how well an individual's sublimatory channels operate—that is, what resources she possesses to generate maximum enjoyment and achievement in all areas of her life and work. Intelligence and skills are significant. The ease with which the individual can articulate his thoughts and emotions, his ability to perceive the relationship between his thoughts, feelings, and actions, and his desire to learn are all important. Education and sociocultural environment play a substantial role in these areas.

The extent to which people are able to cope with their surroundings is closely linked to the quality of their interpersonal relationships, the possession of a secure sense of self, their acceptance of their limitations, and their capacity for reality testing. People who possess more of these qualities rather than fewer will find it easier to deal with the vicissitudes of leadership. They have a greater capacity for self-examination and are able to alternate between action and reflection. Consequently, they are less likely to abuse power and engage in pathological behavior.

The Search for Authenticity

Throughout this book, I have emphasized the need for balance in the relationship between leaders and followers. Unfortunately, balance is particularly vulnerable to the volatility of power, which fuels organizational life; it is all too easily lost. The judicious use of power is crucial to creating common goals and giving meaning to organizational life, but failure to recognize the dual nature of power—that it can be used both constructively and destructively—can affect one's ability to stay in contact with reality. When the sense of balance is lost, political gamesmanship may usurp the focus on organizational effectiveness.

The Roman emperor Marcus Aurelius—no stranger to the vicissitudes of power—warned in his famous *Meditations* that "malice, craftiness, and duplicity are the concomitants of absolute power" (1964, p. 38). Marcus Aurelius's life story shows that he had the strength of character to withstand the darker aspects of power. He was something of a philosopher-king, and his sense of humanity shines through his writings. His reflections on power, which he acted on himself, are still valid today:

> *Men seek for seclusion in the wilderness, by the seashore, or in the mountains—a dream you have cherished only too fondly yourself. But such fancies are wholly unworthy of a philosopher, since at any moment you choose you can retire within yourself. Nowhere can man find a quieter or more untroubled retreat than in his own soul; above all, he who possesses resources in himself, which he need only contemplate to secure immediate ease of mind—the ease that is but another word for well-ordered spirit. Avail yourself often, then, of this retirement, and so continually renew yourself [1964, p. 63].*

Leaders like Marcus Aurelius, however, are rare. Far more often a person who at first sight seems to be well-adjusted changes for the worse when put in a position of power. It is easy to become a sorcerer's apprentice when playing with power. Little is needed for matters to get out of control. In spite of the recurrence of this phenomenon throughout history, social philosophers have often been inclined to ignore it. For example, it can be argued that ideologists such as Marx and Engels, in their search for a just society, were remarkably naive in their assumptions about human nature. Obviously, a similar statement can be made about technocratic ideologists. These human engineers never understood the true nature of the people they were engineering. The complexities of human motivation appear to have been foreign to them. They never seemed to comprehend the pressures of leadership and in particular the addictiveness of power. People who choose to ignore the essence of human nature, and the historical evidence against the abuse of power, do so at their own peril. In this last century we have seen the rise and fall of many dictators and know all too well the terrible price exacted in human suffering for ridding ourselves of them.

Given the psychological make-up of human beings, one of the major aims of society should be the maintenance of a certain balance of power. All too often, and despite the good intentions of their founders, one-party governments have carried within themselves the seeds of their own destruction. All too often the president-for-life phenomenon has ended disastrously. For the purpose of preventive maintenance, situations of balance and counterbalance, of a continuous, constructive disequilibrium, have to be created to avoid the hoarding and subsequent abuse of power by one individual or group of individuals.

In summing up, however, we should not limit ourselves to a discussion of leaders and the kind of safeguards that can be built into organizations in order to keep them in check. Given the fact that we have the responsibility to manage our own life in a sensible, responsible way, we can all be said to be leaders. One way to define success in life is to be able to look back with a sense of satisfaction and not see a series of missed opportunities. Such success requires not only the facility to deal with disappointment but also a creative congruence between one's inner mental state and external circumstances. It demands the strengthening of one's self-reflective, empathic, and listening capacities, and the ready acknowledgment that there are different ways of seeing and understanding. To be a leader means also to be a coach, to take on the role of mentor.

Leaders have to accept the transience of their role and the fact that they have a responsibility to the next generation. A facilitating factor here is the acquisition of a sense of generativity—finding a sense of continuity through others—which will lead to vicarious gratification. Such an attitude will create organizations that learn from experience and will survive.

With this century drawing to a close we can see how leadership by force is increasingly being replaced with leadership by persuasion. More and more people recognize that leadership is a process not only of downward but also of upward influence. Without motivated followers it is hard to be a leader. Authoritarian leadership is being replaced by authoritative leadership. In this process of transformation, self-observation—the ability to monitor one's own performance honestly and critically—is essential. This process of motivation and self-observation requires a basic level of trust and mutual respect. As early as the sixth century B.C. the Chinese sage Lao-tse was aware of the necessity of reciprocity between leaders and followers. He said that the best leader is the one who can enable his followers to say, "We did this ourselves." Leaders, apart from being able to manage themselves, show true leadership if they help others to manage themselves.

Those leaders who are able to combine action with reflection, who have sufficient self-knowledge to recognize the vicissitudes of power, and who will not be tempted away when the psychological sirens that accompany power are beckoning will in the end be the most powerful. They will be the ones who are remembered with respect and affection. They will also be the ones truly able to manage the ambiguities of power and lead a creative and productive life.

references

Aarons, Z. A. "A Study of a Perversion and an Attendant Character Disorder." *Psychoanalytic Quarterly,* 1959, *28*(4), 481–492.

Abraham, K. "The History of an Impostor in the Light of Psychoanalytical Knowledge." In *Clinical Papers on Psychoanalysis.* New York: Brunner/Mazel, 1955. (Originally published 1925.)

Achebe, C. *Ant Hills of the Savanna.* London: Heinemann, 1987.

Aeschylus. *The Persians.* (Philip Vellacott, trans.) Harmondsworth, England: Penguin, 1971.

Ahrens, S., and Deffner, G. "Empirical Study of Alexithymia: Methodology and Results." *American Journal of Psychiatry,* 1986, *40*(3), 430–477.

"Alan Sugar's Professional Foul." *Independent on Sunday* (London), May 24, 1992, p. 20.

Andreas-Salome, L. *Lebensrueckblick* (memoirs). (E. Pfeiffer, ed.) Wiesbaden, Germany: Insel, 1951.

Atchley, R. C. *The Social Forces in Later Life.* Belmont, Calif.: Wadsworth, 1972.

Aurelius, Marcus. *Meditations.* (M. Staniforth, trans.) New York: Viking Penguin, 1964.

Bass, B. M. *Stogdill's Handbook of Leadership.* New York: Free Press, 1981.

Bass, B. M. *Leadership and Performance beyond Expectations.* New York: Free Press, 1985.

Bateson, G. "The Role of Humor in Human Communication." In H. Von Foerster (ed.), *Cybernetics.* New York: Macey Foundation, 1953.

Bennett, N. "Armstrad to Lend Sugar £50m. to Take Firm Private." [London] *Times,* Nov. 6, 1992, p. 27.

Bennis, W., and Nanus, B. *Leaders.* New York: Free Press, 1985.

Bergler, E. "A Clinical Contribution to the Psychogenesis of Humor." *Psychoanalytic Review,* 1937, *24,* 34–53.

Bergman, I. *The Magic Lantern.* London: Hamish Hamilton, 1988.

Bergson, H. *Laughter: An Essay on the Meaning of the Comic.* (C. Bereton and F. Rothwell, trans.) New York: Macmillan, 1928.

Berlyne, D. E. "Laughter, Humor, and Play." In G. Lindzey and E. Aronson (eds.), *Handbook of Social Psychology.* Vol. 3. Reading, Mass.: Addison-Wesley, 1964.

Bettelheim, B. *The Informed Heart.* London: Penguin, 1986.

Bion, W. R. *Experiences in Groups.* London: Tavistock, 1961.

Blanchard, E. B., Arena, J. G., and Pallmeyer, T. P. "Psychosomatic Properties of a Scale to Measure Alexithymia." *Psychotherapy & Psychosomatics,* 1981, *35,* 64–71.

Blum, H. P. "The Psychoanalytic Process and Analytic Inference: A Clinical Study of a Lie and Loss." *International Journal of Psychoanalysis,* 1983, *64,* 17–33.

Bowditch, G. "High Street Midas Who Lost His Golden Touch." [London] *Times,* Jan. 7, 1992, p. 23.

Bower, T. *Maxwell: The Outsider.* London: Mandarin Press, 1991.

Brautigan, B., and Von Rad, M. *Toward a Theory of Psychosomatic Disorders.* Basel: Karger, 1977.

Brooks, G., and Horwitz, T. "As a Gulf War Looms, Saddam's Behavior Grows More Puzzling." *Wall Street Journal,* Jan. 16, 1991, pp. 1–2.

Bullock, A. *Hitler: A Study in Tyranny.* London: Penguin, 1962.

Bunzel, R. L. "Zuni Katcinas." *Bureau of American Ethnology Annual Report,* 47, 1929–1930. Washington, D.C.: Bureau of American Ethnology, 1932.

Burlingham, D. *Twins.* Madison, Conn.: International Universities Press, 1952.

Burns, J. M. *Leadership.* New York: HarperCollins, 1978.

Butler, R. N. "Psychiatry and the Psychology of the Middle Aged." In H. I. Kaplan and B. J. Sadock (eds.), *Comprehensive Textbook of Psychiatry/IV.* (4th ed.) Baltimore, Md.: Williams & Wilkins, 1985.

Camus, A. *La Chute.* (The Fall.) Paris: Gallimar, 1956.

Carlson, D. A. "Dream Mirrors." *Psychoanalytic Quarterly,* 1977, *46*(1), 38–70.

Charles, L. H. "The Clown's Function." *Journal of American Folklore,* 1945, *58,* 25–34.

Clance, P. R. *The Impostor Phenomenon.* New York: Peachtree, 1985.

Clance, P. R., and Imes, S. A. "The Impostor Phenomenon in High-Achieving Women: Dynamics and Therapeutic Intervention." *Psychotherapy: Theory, Research and Practice,* 1978, *15*(3), 241–247.

Cocteau, J. *Orphée.* London: Blackwell, 1976. (Originally published 1926.)

Cohen, R. "Robert Maxwell's Last, Isolated Days." *International Herald Tribune,* Dec. 21–22, 1991, pp. 11, 13.

Cooper, D. *Closer.* New York: Grove-Weidenfeld, 1989.

Crichton, R. *The Great Impostor.* New York: Random House, 1959.

Darwish, A., and Alexander, G. *Unholy Babylon.* London: Victor Gollancz, 1991.

"Days of Reckoning." *Independent* (London), Feb. 10, 1992, p. 20.

Deutsch, H. "The Impostor: Contribution to Ego Psychology of a Type of Psychopath." In *Neuroses and Character Types.* Madison, Conn.: International Universities Press, 1965a. (Originally published 1955.)

Deutsch, H. *Neuroses and Character Types.* Madison, Conn.: International Universities Press, 1965b.

Dowling, C. *The Cinderella Complex.* New York: Summit Books, 1981.

Duncan, W. J. "Humor in Management: Prospects for Administrative Practice and Research." *Academy of Management Review,* 1982, *1*(1), 136–142.

Eisnitz, A. J. "Mirror Dreams." *Journal of the American Psychoanalytic Association,* 1961, *9*, 461–479.

Elkisch, P. "The Psychological Significance of the Mirror."

Journal of the American Psychoanalytic Association, 1957, *5,* 235–244.

Erasmus. *In Praise of Folly.* (B. Radice, trans.; A.H.T. Levine, ed.) Harmondsworth, England: Penguin, 1971. (Originally published 1509.)

Erikson, E. H. *Childhood and Society.* New York: W. W. Norton, 1963.

Erikson, E. H. "Identity and the Life Cycle." *Psychological Issues,* 1959, *1* (entire issue).

Fain, M., and Kreisher, L. "Discussion sur le genese des fonctions représentatives." *Revue Française de Psychanalyse,* 1970, *34,* 285–306.

Feigelson, C. "The Mirror Dream." *Psychoanalytic Study of the Child,* 1975, *30,* 341–355.

Fenichel, O. *The Psychoanalytic Theory of Neurosis.* New York: W. W. Norton, 1945.

Fenichel, O. *The Collected Papers of Otto Fenichel.* (2nd ser.) Madison, Conn.: International Universities Press, 1954.

Fine, R. "Psychoanalysis as a Philosophical System: The Basis for Integrating the Social Sciences." *Journal of Psychohistory,* 1977, *5*(1), 1–65.

Frazer, J. G. *The Golden Bough.* New York: Macmillan, 1947.

Freiberger, H. "Supportive Psychotherapeutic Techniques in Primary and Secondary Alexithymia." *Psychotherapy & Psychosomatics,* 1977, *20,* 337–342.

Freud, A. *The Ego and the Mechanisms of Defense.* (Rev. ed.) Madison, Conn.: International Universities Press, 1966.

Freud, S. "A Case of Hysteria." In J. Strachey (trans. and ed.), *The Standard Edition of the Complete Psychological Works of*

Sigmund Freud. Vol. 7. London: Hogarth Press and Institute of Psychoanalysis, 1953a. (Originally published 1905.)

Freud, S. "Fragment of an Analysis of a Case of Hysteria." In J. Strachey (trans. and ed.), *The Standard Edition of the Complete Psychological Works of Sigmund Freud.* Vol. 7. London: Hogarth Press and Institute of Psychoanalysis, 1953b. (Originally published 1905.)

Freud, S. "Group Psychology and the Analysis of the Ego." In J. Strachey (trans. and ed.), *The Standard Edition of the Complete Psychological Works of Sigmund Freud.* Vol. 18. London: Hogarth Press and Institute of Psychoanalysis, 1953c. (Originally published 1921.)

Freud, S. "Humor." In J. Strachey (trans. and ed.), *The Standard Edition of the Complete Psychological Works of Sigmund Freud.* Vol. 21. London: Hogarth Press and Institute of Psychoanalysis, 1953d. (Originally published 1927.)

Freud, S. "Some Character-Types Met With in Psycho-Analytic Work." In J. Strachey (trans. and ed.), *The Standard Edition of the Complete Psychological Works of Sigmund Freud.* Vol. 14. London: Hogarth Press and Institute of Psychoanalysis, 1953e. (Originally published 1916.)

Freud, S. "Three Essays on the Theory of Sexuality." In J. Strachey (trans. and ed.), *The Standard Edition of the Complete Psychological Works of Sigmund Freud.* Vol. 7. London: Hogarth Press and Institute of Psychoanalysis, 1953f. (Originally published 1905.)

Freud, S. " 'Wild' Psycho-Analysis." In J. Strachey (trans. and ed.), *The Standard Edition of the Complete Psychological Works of Sigmund Freud.* Vol. 11. London: Hogarth Press and Institute of Psychoanalysis, 1953g. (Originally published 1910.)

Freud, S. "Analysis of a Phobia in a Five-Year-Old Boy." In J. Strachey (trans. and ed.), *The Standard Edition of the Complete Psychological Works of Sigmund Freud.* Vol. 10. London: Hogarth Press and Institute of Psychoanalysis, 1955. (Originally published 1909.)

Freud, S. "Civilization and Its Discontents." In J. Strachey (trans. and ed.), *Standard Edition of the Complete Psychological Works of Sigmund Freud.* Vol. 21. London: Hogarth Press and Institute of Psychoanalysis, 1961. (Originally published 1929.)

"From Rags to Riches to Penitentiary." *International Herald Tribune,* July 20, 1989, p. 12.

Fromm, E. *Man for Himself: An Inquiry into the Psychiatry of Ethics.* New York: Fawcett, 1947.

Gardos, G., and others. "Alexithymia: Toward Validation and Measurement." *Comprehensive Psychiatry,* 1984, *25*(3), 278–282.

Gediman, H. K. "Imposture, Inauthenticity and Feeling Fraudulent." *Journal of the American Psychoanalytic Association,* 1985, *33*(4), 911–935.

Geertz, C. *The Interpretation of Culture.* New York: Basic Books, 1973.

Geertz, C. *Local Knowledge.* New York: Basic Books, 1983.

Gillie, O. "Caught Up in Father's Web." *Independent* (London), Dec. 16, 1991, p. 17.

Giscard D'Estaing, V. Quoted in *Economist,* June 8, 1991, p. 110.

Goffman, E. *Interaction Ritual.* New York: Doubleday, Anchor Books, 1967.

Goffman, E. *Relations in Public.* New York: HarperCollins, Colophon Books, 1971.

Gould, R. L. *Transformations.* New York: Simon & Schuster, 1978.

Graff, H. F. "When the Term's Up, It's Better to Go Gracefully." *International Herald Tribune,* Jan. 26, 1988, p. 5.

Greenacre, P. "The Impostor." In *Emotional Growth.* Vol. 1. Madison, Conn.: International Universities Press, 1971a. (Originally published 1958.)

Greenacre, P. "The Relation of the Impostor to the Artist." In *Emotional Growth.* Vol. 2. Madison, Conn.: International Universities Press, 1971b. (Originally published 1958.)

Hanfstängl, E. *The Missing Years.* London: Eyre and Spottiswoode, 1957.

Harrington, A. *Life in a Crystal Palace.* New York: Knopf, 1958.

Harvey-Jones, J. *Making It Happen.* London: Collins, 1988.

Hasek, J. *The Good Soldier Svejk.* (Cecil Parrott, trans.) New York: Crowell, 1972.

Havel, V. *Power of the Powerless.* (J. Keane, ed.) Armonk, N.Y.: M. E. Sharpe, 1990.

Hochschild, A. R. *The Managed Heart.* Berkeley: University of California Press, 1983.

Hodgson, R., Levinson, D. J., and Zaleznik, A. *The Executive Role Constellation.* Boston: Division of Research, Harvard Business School, 1965.

Ibsen, H. *An Enemy of the People.* (R. F. Sharp, trans.) Oxford, England: Oxford University Press, 1988. (Originally published 1882.)

Janis, I. L., and Mann, L. *Decision Making.* New York: Free Press, 1977.

Jaques, E. "Death and the Mid-Life Crises." *International Journal of Psychoanalysis,* 1965, *46,* 502–514.

Jung, C. G. "On the Psychology of the Trickster-Figure." In *The Collected Works of C. G. Jung.* Vol. 9, pt. 1. Princeton, N.J.: Princeton University Press, 1969. (Originally published 1959.)

Kaplan, L. J. "The Concept of the Family Romance." *Psychoanalytic Review,* 1974, *61*(2), 169–202.

Karsh, E., and Rautsi, T. *Saddam Hussein: A Political Biography.* New York: Free Press, 1991.

Kearns, D. *Lyndon Johnson and the American Dream.* New York: HarperCollins, 1976.

Kernberg, O. *Borderline Conditions and Pathological Narcissism.* New York: Aronson, 1975.

Kets de Vries, M.F.R. "Ecological Stress: A Deadly Reminder." *Psychoanalytic Review,* 1980a, *67*(3), 389–408.

Kets de Vries, M.F.R. *Organizational Paradoxes: Clinical Approaches to Management.* London: Tavistock, 1980b.

Kets de Vries, M.F.R. *Prisoners of Leadership.* New York: Wiley, 1989.

Kets de Vries, M.F.R., and Miller, D. *The Neurotic Organization: Diagnosing and Changing Counterproductive Styles of Management.* San Francisco: Jossey-Bass, 1984.

Kets de Vries, M.F.R., and Miller, D. "Narcissism and Leadership: An Object Relations Perspective." *Human Relations,* 1985, *38*(6), 583–601.

Kets de Vries, M.F.R., and Miller, D. "Personality, Culture and Organization." *Academy of Management Review,* 1986, *1*(2), 266–279.

Kets de Vries, M.F.R., and Miller, D. "Interpreting Organizational Texts." *Journal of Management Studies*, 1987, *24*(3), 233–247.

Kets de Vries, M.F.R., and Miller, D. *Unstable at the Top: Inside the Neurotic Organization.* New York: New American Library, 1988.

Kimmel, D. C. *Adulthood and Aging.* New York: Wiley, 1974.

Klapp, O. E. *Heroes, Villains, and Fools.* San Diego, Calif.: Aegis, 1972.

Kohut, H. *The Analysis of the Self.* Madison, Conn.: International Universities Press, 1971.

Kohut, H. *Self Psychology and the Humanities.* New York: W. W. Norton, 1985.

Kotter, J. P. *The General Managers.* New York: Free Press, 1982.

Kris, E. "Ego Development and the Comic." *International Journal of Psychoanalysis*, 1938, *19*, 77–90.

Kris, E. "The Personal Myth: A Problem in Psychoanalytic Technique." In *Selected Papers of Ernst Kris.* New Haven, Conn.: Yale University Press, 1975.

Krystal, H. "Alexithymia and Psychotherapy." *American Journal of Psychotherapy*, 1979, *33*, 17–31.

Krystal, H. "Alexithymia and the Effectiveness of Psychoanalytic Treatment." *International Journal of Psychoanalytic Psychotherapy*, 1982, *9*, 353–378.

Krystal, H. *Massive Psychic Trauma.* Madison, Conn.: International Universities Press, 1986.

Krystal, J. H., Giller, E. L., and Cicchetti, D. V. "Assessment of Alexithymia in Post-traumatic Stress Disorder and Somatic Illness: Introduction of a Reliable Measure." *Psychosomatic Medicine*, 1986, *48*(1/2), 84–94.

Langer, S. K. *Feeling and Form.* London: Routledge & Kegan Paul, 1953.

Lapierre, L. "Mourning, Potency, and Power in Management." *Human Resource Management,* Summer 1989, *28*(2), 177–189.

Lasch, C. *The Culture of Narcissism.* New York: W. W. Norton, 1978.

Leavitt, H. J. *Corporate Pathfinders.* Homewood, Ill.: Dow Jones-Irwin, 1986.

Lehmann, H. E. "Unusual Psychiatric Disorders and Atypical Psychoses." In A. M. Freedman, H. I. Kaplan, and B. J. Sadock (eds.), *Comprehensive Textbook of Psychiatry.* (2nd ed.) Vol. 2. Baltimore, Md.: Williams & Wilkins, 1975.

Leonard, C. "Street Fighter with a Nose for Survival." *Times* (London), Feb. 15, 1992, p. 21.

Lesser, I. M., and Lesser, B. Z. "Alexithymia: Examining the Development of a Psychological Concept." *American Journal of Psychiatry,* 1983, *140*(10), 1305–1308.

Lever, M. *Le sceptre et la marotte.* Paris: Fayard, 1983.

Levine, J. "Regression in Primitive Clowning." *Psychoanalytic Quarterly,* 1961, *30,* 72–83.

Levinson, D. J. *The Seasons of a Man's Life.* New York: Knopf, 1978.

Levinson, H. *Emotional Health in the World of Work.* New York: HarperCollins, 1964.

Lewis, S. *Babbitt.* New York: Harcourt Brace Jovanovich, 1922.

Lowenthal, M., Thurnher, M., and Chiriboga, D. *Four Stages of Life.* San Francisco: Jossey-Bass, 1975.

McClelland, D. C. *The Achieving Society.* New York: Van Nostrand Reinhold, 1961.

Maccoby, M. *The Gamesman.* New York: Simon & Schuster, 1976.

McDougall, J. "The Psychosoma and the Psychoanalytic Process." *International Review of Psychoanalysis,* 1974, *1,* 437–459.

McDougall, J. *Plea for a Measure of Abnormality.* Madison, Conn.: International Universities Press, 1978.

McDougall, J. "The Anti-analysant in Analysis." In S. Lebovici and D. Widlocher (eds.), *Psychoanalysis in France.* Madison, Conn.: International Universities Press, 1980a.

McDougall, J. "A Child Is Being Eaten." *Contemporary Psychoanalysis,* 1980b, *16,* 417–459.

McDougall, J. "Alexithymia: A Psychoanalytic Viewpoint." *Psychotherapy & Psychosomatics,* 1982a, *38,* 81–90.

McDougall, J. "Alexithymia, Psychosomatics, and Psychosis." *International Journal of Psychoanalytic Psychotherapy,* 1982b, *9,* 379–388.

McDougall, J. "The Dis-affected Patient: Reflections on Affect Pathology." *Psychoanalytic Quarterly,* 1984, *53,* 386–409.

McDougall, J. *Theaters of the Body.* New York: W. W. Norton, 1989.

Mahler, M. S. "On Human Symbiosis and the Vicissitudes of Individuation." *Journal of the American Psychoanalytic Association,* 1967, *15,* 740–763.

Mahler, M. S., Pine, F., and Bergman, A. *The Psychological Birth of the Human Infant.* New York: Basic Books, 1975.

Makarius, L., "Le mythe du 'Trickster.'" *Revue de l'histoire des religions,* 1969, *175,* 17–46.

Makarius, L. "Clowns rituels et comportements symboliques." *Diogenes,* 1970, *69,* 47–74.

Makarius, L. "The Crime of Manabozo." *American Anthropologist,* 1973, *75,* 663–675.

Malone, P. "Humor: A Double-Edged Tool for Today's Managers." *Academy of Management Review,* 1980, *5* (3), 357–360.

Martin, J. B., Phil, R. O., and Dobkin, P. "Schalling-Sifneos Personality Scale: Findings and Recommendations." *Psychotherapy & Psychosomatics,* 1984, *41,* 145–152.

Matar, F. *Saddam Hussein: The Man, the Cause and the Future.* London: Third World Center for Research and Publishing, 1981.

Melville, H. *The Confidence Man.* New York: New American Library, 1964. (Originally published 1854.)

Miller, N. G. *The Great Salad Oil Swindle.* Baltimore, Md.: Penguin, 1965.

Muir, K. (ed.). *King Lear.* London: Methuen, 1952.

Myers, W. A. "Imaginary Companions, Fantasy Twins, Mirror Dreams and Depersonalization." *Psychoanalytic Quarterly,* 1976, *45*(4), 503–524.

Neill, J. R., and Sandifer, M. G. "The Clinical Approach to Alexithymia: A Review." *Psychosomatics,* 1982, *23,* 1223–1231.

Nemiah, J. C. "Alexithymia: Theoretical Considerations." *Psychotherapy & Psychosomatics,* 1977, *28,* 199–206.

Nemiah, J. C. "Alexithymia and Psychosomatic Illness." *Journal of Continuing Education in Psychiatry,* 1978, *39,* 25–27.

Nemiah, J. C., and Sifneos, P. E. "Affect and Fantasy in Patients with Psychosomatic Disorders." In O. Hill (ed.), *Modern*

Trends in Psychosomatic Medicine. London: Butterworths, 1970.

Neugarten, B. L. *Personality in Middle and Later Life.* New York: Atherton, 1964.

Neugarten, B. L. (ed.). *Middle Age and Aging: A Reader in Social Psychology.* Chicago: University of Chicago Press, 1968.

Neustadt, R. E. *Presidential Power.* New York: Wiley, 1960.

Olinick, S. L. "Book Review of *The Family Romance of the Imposter-Poet Thomas Chatterton* by Louis G. Kaplan." *Psychoanalytic Quarterly,* 1988, *58*(4), 672–676.

Paolino, T. J. *Psychoanalytic Psychotherapy: Theory, Technique, Therapeutic Relationships and Treatability.* New York: Brunner/Mazel, 1981.

Pollio, H. R., and Edgerly, J. W. "Comedians and Comic Style." In A. J. Chapman and H. C. Frost (eds.), *Humor and Laughter: Theory, Research and Applications.* London: Wiley, 1976.

Proust, M. *Guermantes Way.* (C. K. Scott-Montcrieff, trans.) 1925. (Originally published 1920–1921.)

Racker, H. *Transference and Counter Transference.* Madison, Conn.: International Universities Press, 1968.

Radcliffe-Brown, A. R. *Structure and Function in Primitive Society.* London: Cohen and West, 1952.

Radin, P. *Trickster: A Study in American Indian Mythology.* Westport, Conn.: Greenwood, 1969. (Originally published 1956.)

Rayski, B. "Saddam Hussein." *Globe,* Mar. 1991, pp. 12–23.

Reik, T. *Masochism in Modern Man.* New York: Farrer & Rinehart, 1941.

Roheim, G. *Spiegelzauber.* Vienna: International Psychoanalytic Verlag, 1919.

Rosovsky, H. *The University: An Owner's Manual.* New York: W. W. Norton, 1990.

Ross, J. M., and others. *Father and Child.* Boston: Little, Brown, 1982.

Roy, D. F. "Banana Time: Job Satisfaction and Informal Interaction." *Human Organization,* 1960, *18,* 158–168.

Schafer, R. "The Pursuit of Failure and the Idealization of Unhappiness." *American Psychologist,* 1984, *39*(4), 398–405.

Scott, C. "Who Is Afraid of Wilfred Bion?" Unpublished paper, Canadian Psychoanalytic Society, 1980.

Shakespeare, W. *Richard III.* In W. G. Clark and W. A. Wright (eds.), *The Complete Works of William Shakespeare.* Vol. 1. New York: Doubleday, 1988.

Shaw, G. B. *Candida.* Chicago: Nelson-Hall, 1973. (Originally published 1893.)

Shengold, L. "The Metaphor of the Mirror." *Journal of the American Psychoanalytic Association,* 1974, *22*(1), 97–115.

Shipko, S., Alvarez, W. A., and Norrello, N. "Towards a Teleological Model of Alexithymia: Alexithymia and Post-traumatic Stress Disorder." *Psychotherapy and Psychosomatics,* 1983, *39,* 122–126.

Sonnenfeld, J. "Heroes in Collision: Chief Executive Retirement and the Parade of Future Leaders." *Human Resource Management,* Summer 1986, *25*(2), 305–333.

Speer, A. *Inside the Third Reich.* New York: Avon, 1970.

Speer, A. *Spandau: The Secret Diaries.* New York: Macmillan, 1976.

Spence, D. *Narrative Truth and Historical Truth.* New York: W. W. Norton, 1982.

Steward, J. H. "The Ceremonial Buffoon of the American Indian." In *Papers of the Michigan Academy of Science, Arts, and Letters.* Vol. 14. Ann Arbor: University of Michigan, 1931.

Sundqvist, S.-I. *Refaat & Fermenta: Dramat och Aktörerna.* Stockholm: Författarfölaget, 1987.

Swain, B. *Fools and Folly during the Middle Ages and the Renaissance.* New York: Columbia University Press, 1932.

Swanson, D. A. "The Münchhausen Syndrome." *American Journal of Psychotherapy,* 1981, *35*(3), 436–444.

Tapie, B. *Gagner.* (Winning.) Paris: Robert Laffont, 1986.

Taylor, G. J. "Alexithymia and the Counter-transference." *Psychotherapy & Psychosomatics,* 1977, *28*, 141–147.

Taylor, G. J. "Alexithymia: Concept, Measurement, and Implications for Treatment." *American Journal of Psychiatry,* 1984, *141*(6), 725–732.

Thompson, P., and Delano, A. *Maxwell: A Portrait of Power.* London: Corgi, 1988.

Tichy, N. M., and Devanna, M. A. *The Transformational Leader.* New York: Wiley, 1986.

Vaillant, G. E. *Adaptation to Life.* Boston: Little, Brown, 1977.

Von Rad, M. *Alexithymie, Empirische Untersuchen zur Diagnostik und Therapie Psychosomatische Kranker.* Berlin: Springer Verlag, 1983.

Von Rad, M. "Alexithymia and Symptom Formation." *Psychotherapy & Psychosomatics,* 1984, *42*, 80–89.

Waller, M. "Ratner Quits the Family Firm: Chief Executive

Pays Price for Attracting Bad Publicity." *Times* (London), Nov. 26, 1992, p. 21.

Weber, M. *The Theory of Social and Economic Organization.* (A. M. Henderson and T. Parsons, trans.) New York: Oxford University Press, 1947.

Weinshel, E. M. "Some Observations on Not Telling the Truth." *Journal of the American Psychoanalytic Association,* 1979, *27*(3), 503–532.

Wells, K., Bray, N., and Reilly, P. M. "Maxwell Empire's Assets Go On Sale with Hopes of Covering Huge Debt." *Wall Street Journal,* Dec. 6, 1991, p. 3.

Welsford, E. *The Fool.* London: Faber and Faber, 1935.

Whyte, W. H. *The Organization Man.* New York: Simon & Schuster, 1956.

Wilde, O. *The Picture of Dorian Gray.* New York: Random House, 1992. (Originally published 1890.)

Winnicott, D. W. *Playing and Reality.* New York: Basic Books, 1971.

Winnicott, D. W. *Through Paediatrics to Psychoanalysis.* New York: Basic Books, 1975.

Wittebort, S. "Behind the Great Swedish Scandal." *Institutional Investor,* Aug. 1987, pp. 93–104.

Zaleznik, A. *The Managerial Mystique.* New York: HarperCollins, 1989.

selected readings

Abraham, K. *Selected Papers on Psychoanalysis.* New York: Basic Books, 1968.

Adams, J. S. "Toward an Understanding of Equity." *Journal of Abnormal and Social Psychology,* Nov. 1963, 422–436.

Adler, A. *Study of Organ Inferiority and Its Physical Compensation.* New York: Nervous and Mental Disease Publishing Co., 1917. (Originally published 1907.)

American Psychiatric Association. *Diagnostic and Statistical Manual of Mental Disorders, DSM IIIR.* (Rev. ed.) Washington, D.C.: American Psychiatric Association, 1987.

Augustine of Hippo. *Confessions.* Harmondsworth, England: Penguin, 1961.

Barnard, C. J. *The Functions of the Executive.* Cambridge, Mass.: Harvard University Press, 1938.

Bers, S. A., and Rodin, J. "Social-Comparison Jealousy: A Developmental and Motivational Study." *Journal of Personality and Social Psychology,* 1984, *47*(4), 766–779.

Bhide, A., and Stevenson, H. "Why Be Honest If Honesty

Doesn't Pay." In *Ethics at Work.* Cambridge, Mass.: Harvard Business Review, 1991.

Bion, W. R. "Attention and Interpretation." In *Seven Servants: Four Works by Wilfred R. Bion.* New York: Aronson, 1977.

Block, S. "Humor in Group Therapy." In W. F. Frye, Jr., and W. A. Salameh (eds.), *Handbook of Humor and Psychotherapy.* Sarasota, Fla.: Professional Resources Exchange, 1987.

Bortenfall, B. I., and Fischer, K. W. "Development of Self-Recognition in the Infant." *Developmental Psychology,* 1978, *14,* 44–50.

Bradney, P. "The Joking Relationships in Industry." *Human Relations,* 1957, *10,* 179–187.

Breuer, J., and Freud, S. "Studies on Hysteria." In J. Strachey (trans. and ed.), *The Standard Edition of the Complete Psychological Works of Sigmund Freud.* Vol. 2. London: Hogarth Press and Institute of Psychoanalysis, 1953. (Originally published 1893–1895.)

Bromberg, N. "Hitler's Childhood." *International Review of Psycho-analyses,* 1974, *1,* 227–234.

Buchanan, S. "Firms Bring on the Clowns to Act Out Their Problems." *International Herald Tribune,* Dec. 1, 1988, p. 9.

Burlingham, D. *Twins.* Madison, Conn.: International Universities Press, 1952.

Burns, T., and Stalker, G. M. *The Management of Innovation.* London: Tavistock, 1961.

Burrell, G. "Sex and Organizational Analysis." *Organization Studies,* 1904, *5*(2), 97–118.

Bursten, B. *The Manipulator: A Psychoanalytic View.* New

Haven, Conn., and London: Yale University Press, 1973.

Butler, R. N., and Lewis, M. I. *Aging and Mental Health.* St. Louis, Mo.: Mosby, 1977.

Calder, B. J. "An Attribution Theory of Leadership." In B. M. Staw and G. R. Salancik (eds.), *New Directions in Organizational Behavior.* Chicago: St. Clair Press, 1977.

Castelnuovo-Tedesco, P. "Stealing, Revenge and the Monte Cristo Complex." *International Journal of Psychoanalysis,* 1974, *55,* 169–177.

Castelnuovo-Tedesco, P. "Psychological Consequences of Physical Defects: A Psychoanalytical Perspective." *International Review of Psychoanalysis,* 1981, *8,* 145–154.

Chaplin, C. *My Autobiography.* New York: Simon & Schuster, 1964.

Churchill, W. S. *The Second World War.* Vol. 6: *Triumph and Tragedy.* Boston: Houghton-Mifflin, 1953.

Churchill, W. S. *Painting as a Pastime.* Harmondsworth, England: Penguin, 1964.

Coen, S. J., and Bradlow, P. A. "The Common Mirror Dream, Dreamer, and the Dream Mirror." *Journal of the American Psychoanalytic Association,* 1985, *3*(4), 797–820.

Connellan, T. K. *How to Improve Performance: Behaviorism in Business.* New York: HarperCollins, 1978.

Davies, A. F. *Skills, Outlooks and Passions.* Cambridge, England: Cambridge University Press, 1980.

de M'Uzan, M. "Analytical Process and the Notion of the Past." *International Review of Psychoanalysis,* 1974, *1,* 461–466.

Desmond, A. *The Ape's Reflection.* London: Quartet Books, 1980.

Deutsch, H. "Some Forms of Emotional Disturbance and Their Relationship to Schizophrenia." In *Neuroses and Character Types.* Madison, Conn.: International Universities Press, 1965. (Originally published 1942.)

DeVore, I. *Primate Behavior: Field Studies of Monkeys and Apes.* New York: Holt, Rinehart & Winston, 1965.

Dupont, R. L. "The Impostor and His Mother." *Journal of Nervous and Mental Disease,* 1970, *150*(6), 444–448.

Erikson, E. H. *Identity, Youth and Crisis.* New York: W. W. Norton, 1968.

Fast, I. "A Function of Action in the Early Development of Identity." *International Journal of Psychoanalysis,* 1970, *51,* 471–478.

Finkelstein, L. "The Impostor: Aspects of His Development." *Psychoanalytic Quarterly,* 1974, *43*(1), 85–114.

Fisher, S., and Fisher, R. L. *Pretend the World Is Funny and Forever: A Psychological Analysis of Comedians, Clowns, and Actors.* Hillsdale, N.J.: Erlbaum, 1981.

Fossey, D. *Gorillas in the Mist.* Boston: Houghton Mifflin, 1983.

Foster, G. M. "The Anatomy of Envy: A Study in Symbolic Behavior." *Current Anthropology,* 1972, *13*(2), 165–202.

Frankel, S., and Sherick, I. "Observations on the Development of Normal Envy." *Psychoanalytic Study of the Child,* 1977, *32,* 257–281.

Freud, S. "The Dynamics of Transference." In J. Strachey (trans. and ed.), *The Standard Edition of the Complete Psychological Works of Sigmund Freud.* Vol. 12. London: Hogarth Press and Institute of Psychoanalysis, 1953. (Originally published 1912.)

Freud, S. "Jokes and Their Relation to the Unconscious." In J.

Strachey (trans. and ed.), *The Standard Edition of the Complete Psychological Works of Sigmund Freud.* Vol. 8. London: Hogarth Press and Institute of Psychoanalysis, 1953. (Originally published 1905.)

Freud, S. "Some Psychological Consequences of the Anatomical Distinction between the Sexes." In J. Strachey (trans. and ed.), *The Standard Edition of the Complete Psychological Works of Sigmund Freud.* Vol. 19. London: Hogarth Press and Institute of Psychoanalysis, 1953. (Originally published 1925.)

Fry, W. F., and Allen, M. *Make 'Em Laugh.* Palo Alto, Calif.: Science and Behavior Books, 1975.

Gallup, G. G. "Chimpanzees: Self-Recognition." *Science,* 1970, *167,* 86–87.

Giscard D'Estaing, V. *Le pouvoir et la vie.* Vol. 11: *L'affrontement.* Paris: Compagnie 12, 1991.

Gittings, R. *John Keats.* London: Penguin, 1971.

Gottdiener, A. "The Impostor." *Contemporary Psychoanalysis,* 1982, *18*(3), 438–454.

Grand, H. G. "The Masochistic Defense of the 'Double Mask': Its Relationship to Imposture." *International Journal of Psychoanalysis,* 1973, *54,* 445–454.

Green, S. G., and Mitchell, T. R. "Attributional Processes of Leaders in Leader-Member Interactions." *Organizational Behavior and Human Performance,* 1979, *23,* 429–458.

Greenson, R. R. "On Screen Defenses, Screen Hunger, and Screen Identity." *Journal of the American Psychoanalytic Association,* 1958, *6,* 242–262.

Groen, J. A. *Afgunst regeert de wereld.* Amsterdam: Boom, 1986.

Grossman, W. I. "Notes on Masochism: A Discussion of the

History and Development of a Psychoanalytic Concept." *Psychoanalytic Quarterly,* 1986, *55*(3), 379–413.

Hackman, J. R. "The Psychology of Self-Management in Organizations." In M. S. Pollack and R. O. Perloff (eds.), *Psychology and Work: Productivity Change and Employment.* Washington, D.C.: American Psychological Association, 1986.

Herzberg, F. "One More Time: How Do You Motivate Employees?" *Harvard Business Review,* 1968, *46,* 53–62.

Herzberg, F., Mausner, B., and Snyderman, B. *The Motivation to Work.* New York: Wiley, 1959.

Hitler, A. *Mein Kampf.* Boston: Houghton Mifflin, 1943. (Originally published 1924.)

Hoffmann, E.T.A. *The Best Tales of Hoffmann.* Mineola, N.Y.: Dover, 1967.

Homans, G. *Social Behavior: Its Elementary Forms.* Orlando, Fla.: Harcourt Brace Jovanovich, 1961.

Horney, K. "The Value of Vindictiveness." *American Journal of Psychoanalysis,* 1948, *8,* 3–12.

Horney, K. "The Flight from Womanhood: The Masculinity Complex in Women as Viewed by Men and Women." In *Feminine Psychology.* New York: W. W. Norton, 1967.

Iacocca, L. *Iacocca: An Autobiography.* New York: Bantam Books, 1984.

Iacocca, L. "Iacocca." *Fortune,* Aug. 29, 1988, pp. 24–29.

Jerusalem Bible. (Reader's ed.) New York: Doubleday, 1966.

Joffe, W. G. "A Critical Review of the Status of the Envy Concept." *International Journal of Psychoanalysis,* 1969, *50,* 533–545.

Johnson, A. M., and Szurek, S. A. "The Genesis of Antisocial Acting Out in Children and Adults." *Psychoanalytic Quarterly,* 1952, *21,* 323–343.

Jung, C. G. *The Archetypes and the Collective Unconscious.* Bollinger Series 20. Princeton, N.J.: Princeton University Press, 1959.

Kant, I. *Metaphysik der Sitten.* In K. Vorlander (ed.), *Samtliche Werke.* (4th ed.) Vol. 3. Leipzig: Kröner Verlag, 1922. (Originally published 1959.)

Karme, L. "A Clinical Report on Penis Envy: Its Multiple Meanings and Defensive Function." *Journal of the American Psychoanalytic Association,* 1981, *29*(2), 427–446.

Kets de Vries, M.F.R. "The Dark Side of Entrepreneurship." *Harvard Business Review,* Nov.-Dec, 1985, pp. 160–167.

Kets de Vries, M.F.R. "The Dark Side of CEO Succession." *Harvard Business Review,* Jan.-Feb. 1988, pp. 56–61.

Klein, M. "A Contribution to the Psychogenesis of Manic-Depressive States." In *Contributions to Psychoanalysis, 1921–1945.* New York: McGraw-Hill, 1964. (Originally published 1935.)

Klein, M. *Envy and Gratitude and Other Works 1946–1963.* New York: Delta Books, 1965.

Klein, M. *Love, Guilt and Reparation and Other Works 1921–1945.* London: Virago, 1988.

Knapp, P. H. (ed.). *Expression of Emotions in Man.* Madison, Conn.: International Universities Press, 1963.

Knapp, P. H. "The Mysterious Split: An Inquiry into the Mind-Body Relationship." In G. Globus, G. Maxwell, and J.

Savodnik (eds.), *Consciousness and the Brain.* New York: Plenum, 1976.

Köhler, W. *The Mentality of Apes.* Harmondsworth, England: Penguin, 1957.

Kohut, H. "The Psychoanalytic Treatment of Narcissistic Personality Disorders." In *The Psychoanalytic Study of the Child.* Vol. 23. Madison, Conn.: International Universities Press, 1968.

Kohut, H. *The Restoration of the Self.* Madison, Conn.: International Universities Press, 1977.

Kohut, H., and Wolf, E. S. "The Disorders of the Self and Their Treatment: An Outline." *International Journal of Psychoanalysis,* 1978, *59,* 413–426.

Kosinski, J. *Being There.* New York: Bantam Books, 1972.

Krystal, H. *Massive Psychic Trauma.* Madison, Conn.: International Universities Press, 1968.

Krystal, H. "The Genetic Development of Affects and Affect Regression." *Annual of Psychoanalysis,* pt. 2, 1974, pp. 98–126.

Krystal, H. *Integration and Self-Healing.* Hillsdale, N.J.: Analytic Press, 1988.

Lacan, J. "Le stade du miroir comme formateur de la fonction du Je, telle qu'elle nous est révélée dans l'expérience psychoanalytique." *Revue Française de Psychanalyse,* 1949, *13,* 449–455.

Lacan, J. *Ecrits.* (A. Sheridan, trans.) London: Tavistock, 1977.

Langs, R. *The Therapeutic Interaction.* 2 vols. New York: Aronson, 1976.

Lazarus, R. S. "Thoughts on the Relations between Emotion

and Cognition." *American Psychologist,* 1982, *37,* 1019–1024.

Lichtenstein, H. "The Role of Narcissism in the Emergence and Maintenance of Primary Identity." *International Journal of Psychoanalysis,* 1964, *45,* 49–56.

Lichtenstein, H. "Narcissism and Primary Identity." In *The Dilemma of Human Identity.* New York: Aronson, 1977.

Locke, E. A., and Bryan, J. F. "Goal-Setting as a Determinant of the Effect of Knowledge of Score on Performance." *American Journal of Psychology,* 1968, *8,* 398–406.

Lord, R. G., and Smith, J. E. "Theoretical Information Processing and Situational Factors Affecting Attribution Theory Models of Organizational Behavior." *Academy of Management Review,* 1983, *8*(1), 50–60.

Luborsky, L., and others. "A Verification of Freud's Grandest Clinical Hypothesis: The Transference." *Clinical Psychology Review,* 1985, *5,* 231–246.

Luborsky, L., Crits-Cristoph, P., Minz, J., and Auerbach, A. *Who Will Benefit from Psychotherapy?* New York: Basic Books, 1988.

Luthans, F., and Kreitner, R. *Organizational Behavior Modification.* Glenview, Ill.: Scott, Foresman, 1975.

Machiavelli, N. *The Prince.* (R. M. Adams, trans.) New York: W. W. Norton, 1977. (Originally published 1532.)

Mann, T. *Confessions of Felix Krull, Confidence Man.* New York: Random House, Vintage Books, 1969. (Originally published 1954.)

Manz, C. C., and Sims, H. P., Jr. "Self-Management as a Substitute for Leadership: A Social Learning Theory Perspective." *Academy of Management Review,* 1980, *5*(3), 361–367.

Manz, C. C., and Sims, H. P., Jr. "Leading Workers to Lead Themselves: The External Leadership of Self-Managing Work Teams." *Administrative Science Quarterly,* 1987, *32,* 106–128.

Martin, J. "Clinical Contributions to the Theory of the Fictive Personality." *Annual of Psychoanalysis,* 1985, *12/13,* 267–300.

Martin, J. *Who Am I This Time: Uncovering the Fictive Personality.* New York: W. W. Norton, 1988.

Marty, P., and de M'Uzan, M. "La pensée opératoire." *Revue Française de Psychanalyse,* 1963, *27,* 1345–1354.

Maslow, A. *Motivation and Personality.* New York: HarperCollins, 1954.

Masters, W. H., and Johnson, V. E. *Human Sexual Inadequacy.* Boston: Little, Brown, 1970.

Mathews, M. C. "Whistleblowing: Acts of Courage Are Often Discouraged." *Business and Society Review,* 1987, *63,* 40–44.

Mazlish, B. "Leader and Led; Individual and Group." *Psychohistory Review,* 1981, *9*(3), 214–237.

Meindl, J. R., Ehrlich, S. B., and Dukerich, J. M. "The Romance of Leadership." *Administrative Science Quarterly,* 1985, *30,* 78–102.

Meltzoff, D. "Immediate and Deferred Imitation in 14- and 24-Month-Old Infants." *Child Development,* 1985, *56,* 62–72.

Merleau-Ponty, M. *The Primacy of Perception: And Other Essays on Phenomenological Psychology, the Philosophy of Art, His-*

tory, and Politics. (J. M. Edie and others, trans. and eds.) Evanston, Ill.: Northwestern University Press, 1964.

Miller, A. *Prisoners of Childhood.* New York: Basic Books, 1981.

Mills, P. K. "Self-Management: Its Control and Relationship to Other Organizational Properties." *Academy of Management Review,* 1983, *8*(3), 445–453.

Niederland, W. G. "Narcissistic Ego Impairment in Patients with Early Physical Malformations." *Psychoanalytic Study of the Child,* 1965, *20*, 518.

Noy, P. C. "A Revision of the Psychoanalytic Theory of Affect." *Annual of Psychoanalysis,* 1982, *10*, 139–186.

Oppenheimer, P. *A Pleasant Vintage of Till Eulenspiegel.* Middletown, Conn.: Wesleyan University Press, 1972.

Osten, S. *Hitler's Barndom.* (Hitler's Childhood.) Stockholm: Folmer Hansen, 1984.

Payne, R. *Hubris: A Study of Pride.* New York: HarperCollins, 1960.

Pfeffer, J. "The Ambiguity of Leadership." *Academy of Management Review,* 1977, *2*, 104–112.

Phillips, J. S., and Lord, R. G. "Causal Attributions and Perceptions of Leadership." *Organizational Behavior and Human Performance,* 1981, *28*, 143–163.

Pines, M. "Reflections on Mirroring." *International Review of Psychoanalysis,* 1984, *11*, 27–42.

Plato. *The Republic.* (H.D.P. Lee, trans.) Harmondsworth, England: Penguin, 1955.

Plutchick, R. *Emotion: A Psycho-evolutionary Synthesis.* New York: HarperCollins, 1980.

Porter, R. "The Language of Quackery in England." In P. Burke and R. Porter (eds.), *The Social History of Language.* Cambridge, England: Cambridge University Press, 1987.

Reich, A. "Narcissistic Object Choice in Women." *Journal of the American Psychoanalytic Association,* 1953, *1,* 22–24.

Rilke, R. M. *The Notebooks of Malte Laurids Brigge.* (M. D. Herter Norton, trans.) New York: W. W. Norton, 1949. (Originally published 1910.)

Rochlin, G. *Griefs and Discontents.* Boston: Little, Brown, 1965.

Romanyshyn, R. D. *Psychological Life: From Science to Metaphor.* Bristol, Penn.: Open University Press, 1982.

Rose, G. J. "King Lear and the Use of Humor in Treatment." *Journal of the American Psychoanalytic Association,* 1969, *17,* 927–940.

Rosenblatt, A. D. "Envy, Identification and Pride." *Psychoanalytic Quarterly,* 1988, *57,* 56–72.

Ross, N. "The 'As If' Concept." *Journal of the American Psychoanalytic Association,* 1967, *15*(1), 59–82.

Schein, E. H. "Reassessing the 'Divine Rights' of Managers." *Sloan Management Review,* Winter 1989, pp. 63–68.

Schoeck, H. *Envy: A Theory of Social Behavior.* New York: Harcourt Brace Jovanovich, 1969.

Sculley, J., and Byrne, J. A. *Odyssey.* New York: HarperCollins, 1987.

Searles, H. F. *Collected Papers on Schizophrenia and Related Subjects.* Madison, Conn.: International Universities Press. 1965.

Shoumatoff, A. *African Madness.* New York: Knopf, 1988.

Shulman, D. G. "Narcissism in Two Forms: Implications for the Practicing Psychoanalyst." *Psychoanalytic Psychology,* 1986, *3*(2), 133–147.

Sifneos, P. E. *Short-Term Psychotherapy and Emotional Crisis.* Cambridge, Mass.: Harvard University Press, 1972.

Sifneos, P. E. "The Prevalence of Alexithymic Characteristics in Psychosomatic Patients." *Psychotherapy & Psychosomatics,* 1973, *22,* 255–262.

Silver, M., and Sabini, J. "The Social Construction of Envy." *Journal of the Theory of Social Behavior,* 1978, *8*(3), 313–332.

Simons, R. C. "Psychoanalytic Contribution to Psychiatric Nosology: Forms of Masochistic Behavior." *Journal of the American Psychoanalytic Association,* 1987, *35*(3), 583–608.

Skinner, B. F. *Science and Human Behavior.* New York: Free Press, 1953.

Skinner, B. F. *About Behaviorism.* New York: Knopf, 1976.

Smeltzer, L. R., and Leap, T. L. "An Analysis of Individual Reactions to Potentially Offensive Jokes in Work Settings." *Human Relations,* 1988, *41,* 295–303.

Sonnenfeld, J. *The Hero's Farewell.* New York: Oxford University Press, 1988.

Speilman, P. M. "Envy and Jealousy: An Attempt at Clarification." *Psychoanalytic Quarterly,* 1971, *40,* 59–82.

Storr, A. *The Art of Psychotherapy.* London: Methuen, 1979.

Sullivan, H. S. *The Interpersonal Theory of Psychiatry.* New York: W. W. Norton, 1953.

Tellenbach, H. "On the Nature of Jealousy." *Journal of Phenomenological Psychology,* 1974, *4*(2), 461–468.

Titelman, P. "A Phenomenological Comparison between Envy and Jealousy." *Journal of Phenomenological Psychology,* 1981, *12*(2), 189–204.

Ulanov, A., and Ulanov, B. *Cinderella and Her Sisters.* Philadelphia: Westminster Press, 1983.

Vancil, R. F. *Passing the Baton: Managing the Process of CEO Succession.* Boston: Harvard Business School Press, 1987.

Volkogonov, D. *The Stalin Phenomenon.* Moscow: Novesti Press Agency Publishing House, 1988.

Vroom, V. H. *Work and Motivation.* New York: Wiley, 1964.

Walton, R. E. "From Control to Commitment in the Workplace." *Harvard Business Review,* 1985, *63*(2), 77–84.

Weiss, J. "Clinical and Theoretical Aspects of 'As If' Characters." *Journal of the American Psychoanalytic Association,* 1966, *14,* 569–590.

Welch, J. Speech given in 1981 at the Harvard Business School. Video ICH 9-181-111. Cambridge, Mass.: President and Fellows of Harvard College, 1982.

Wijsenbeek, H., and Nitzan, I. "The Case of Peter, an Impostor." *Psychiatra, Neurologia, Neurochirurgia,* 1968, *71,* 193–202.

Willeford, W. *The Fool and His Scepter.* Chicago: Northwestern University Press, 1969.

Zajonc, R. B. "Feeling and Thinking: Preferences Need No Inferences." *American Psychologist,* 1980, *35,* 151–157.

Zajonc, R. B. "On the Primacy of Affect." *American Psychologist,* 1984, *39,* 117–123.

Zaleznik, A., and Kets de Vries, M.F.R. *Power and the Corporate Mind.* Chicago: Bonus Books, 1985.

Zuboff, S. *In the Age of the Smart Machine.* New York: Basic Books, 1988.

index